Principled Profit: Marketing That Puts People First

Many of these blurbs are shortened for space reasons (some were quite long). The complete versions are posted at <http://www.principledprofits.com/blurbs.html>

"People **want** to change the paradigm toward cooperation and people-centered behavior.... They can profit handsomely by doing so. I'm delighted to recommend this book."

Jack Canfield, CEO, Chicken Soup for the Soul Enterprises, co-author, *Chicken Soup for the Soul at Work*

"A welcome change from the scandals in the business pages. It's everything you need to make a very nice livelihood and still feel pride when you look in the mirror."

Jim Hightower, "America's #1 Populist," author of *There's Nothing in the Middle of the Road but Yellow Stripes and Dead Armadillos* and other books, former Texas Commissioner of Agriculture

"Highly practical.... These real-life business stories are useful for every CEO who wants to grow sustainable profits."

Anne Holland, publisher, MarketingSherpa, Inc.

"Shel Horowitz's call for ethics in the business world is just as relevant to the world of public management and politics. It's all about serving the people with integrity and care."

Robert B. Reich, Former U.S. Secretary of Labor, and professor, Brandeis University

"Shel Horowitz's superb book gives you the equivalent of an MBA in the people business. You're going to love it and people are going to love you."

Jay Conrad Levinson, author, *Guerrilla Marketing* series of books

"It's the overall approach, the adjustment that it will make in your mindset, that is so important.... Make the difference between leading a stress-filled 'what's wrong' existence and a bountiful 'business is a joy' life."

Dr. Ken Evoy, president, SiteSell.com

"Shows, on every page, that not only is it possible to succeed by appealing to the good side of human nature, but that the resulting success is easier to achieve and more satisfying."

Mary Westheimer, president, Bookzone.com

"No message could be more timely than Shel Horowitz's. In the long run, only an ethical approach to marketing works."

Al Ries, co-author, *The Fall of Advertising and the Rise of PR*

"An exceptional and well-researched book that is totally in line with the way I have done business in the last 29 years. I urge every business owner, every speaker, and

every serious student of marketing or psychology to buy it."
Tom Antion, small business Internet marketing expert

"Nothing held back, non-traditional, straight-shooting, and creative solutions."
Azriela Jaffe, syndicated business columnist and author of thirteen books

"It's common in business to use the bludgeon of money to attempt to meet challenges.... Horowitz has employed the more sophisticated tools of intelligence, ethics, cooperation, ingenuity and creativity."
John Audette, publisher, Adventive

"Shows ethical and nice isn't just about being a good guy—it's about getting the biggest bang for your buck and the largest return on effort and investment. If you're interested in success, you need to read this book."
Sheldon Bowles, co-author with Ken Blanchard of Raving Fans
and three other books

"Combines the best of marketing and relationship theory with real-world examples and practical advice."
Melanie Rigney, editor, Writer's Digest magazine, editorial director,
Writer's Digest Trade Books

"Bold, usable approaches that fly in the face of traditional and sometimes unethical business wisdom."
Brian Jud, author, speaker, marketing strategist

"Shel Horowitz has got it right.... The bigger the competitor you team up with, the greater the chance that you'll end up with some of the business they can't handle."
B. L. Ochman, marketing strategist, journalist, speaker

"Paints a picture of a business world populated by real human beings ... who've discovered their competitors are really collaborators; and their threats are really opportunities. People who've learnt to do well while doing good."
Simon Young, managing director, Simon Young Writers,
Auckland, New Zealand

"The entrepreneur's best friend and companion when it comes to taking action steps to fame."
Marisa D'Vari, president, Deg.Com Communications

"Succinct and practical ... lean but not mean, face to face without being in your face.... Succeed without losing identity and integrity."
Ira Bryck, director, University of Massachusetts Family Business Center

You have a complete command of marketing techniques and the psychology behind it.... If you put people first, you **will** win in business!"
Kristie Tamsevicius, author, I Love My Life, WebMomz.com, teacher, consultant

"'Honesty...can be used to increase business, promote your brand, retain customers and easily attract new ones at far less cost."

Walt Boyes, principal, Spitzer and Boyes LLC, author, columnist, speaker,

"Overflowing with creative, innovative and fun ideas to help you market yourself, your products and services inexpensively, effectively and ethically."

Susan Z. Martin, Where Can I Buy A Car Online

"Shows you **how** to build mutually beneficial and profitable relationships not only with customers, but with employees, suppliers, and even competitors.... Powerful and profitable. A terrific and long-overdue book."

Eric Gelb, MBA & CPA, author, *Book Promotion Made Easy* and editor, *Publishing Gold* e-zine

"As usual, you packed a lot of ideas into a compact, tightly written book. My favorite bit of advice: Get paid to do your marketing."

Martha Retallick, owner, LRP Designs

"Will not only help you to make lots of money, but to feel great while doing so.... The money you make is directly proportionate to how many people you serve and how well you serve them."

Bob Burg, author of *Endless Referrals* and *Winning Without Intimidation*

"A must read for anyone who wants to understand the new way of doing business and doing it well."

John Kremer, author, *1001 Ways to Market Your Books*

"How to be highly successful and still sleep at night.... A jewel of a book."

Lorilyn Bailey, CEO, NewsBuzz.com

"Ruthless, winner-takes-all marketing strategies...are destructive to your business.... Dozens of easy-to-implement, low-cost honest marketing tactics that, in Shel's own words... 'not only feel better but work better.'"

David Frey, president, Marketing Best Practices

"Keep it handy on your favorite bookshelf. Use it to plan your marketing strategies year after year.... Grow your business with a lot less effort."

Denise O'Berry, The Small Business Edge

"Should be required reading in business schools so that we can avoid another headline-grabbing avalanche of corporate misdeeds."

Harry Hoover, managing principal, Hoover Ink PR

"Focuses on ... ethical standards, building relationships and providing quality services. Filled with interesting and applicable tips, personal stories and examples."

Melanie Rembrandt, owner, Rembrandt Communications

"One of the best books I've read on marketing...in a long time....Focuses very strongly on success coming from making the lives of everyone else better, rather than stepping on your neighbor to 'move up the ladder.'"

Josh Samuels, Melaleuca Independent Distributor

"Shows marketers how ethical marketing practices generate long-term paybacks through consumer relationships that last."

Mona Doyle, The Consumer Network, Inc.

"Eminently readable and full of real-world examples that not only will instruct but also will inspire the reader."

Steve Yankee, writer, consultant, workshop leader

"In an age of Enron ethics and Worldcom cons, it's refreshing to read a book that clearly demonstrates the value of virtue. Based on research findings, case studies and his own business practices, Shel Horowitz shows us that straight shooting and long-term business success are not antithetical."

Yvette Borcia, partner, Stern & Associates, co-editor, *Stern's Management Review*, co-author, *Stern's SourceFinder* and *All About Pay*

"Business growth [is] not based on a zero sum game. Your gaining of market share doesn't necessarily mean loss of market share for your competitors....Principles...that have built business leaders like Nordstrom, Avis, and Saturn."

Jim Deitz, The Franchise Doctor

"I am gratified to see a book promoting business ethics, produced by an author of this caliber. This should be required reading in all business curricula."

Eva Rosenberg, MBA, publisher, TaxMama.com, noted financial and Internet speaker

"The most successful companies...create value for the customer. I wish all marketing strategies were based upon Shel's Magic Triangle of Quality, Integrity, and Honesty."

Peter Hupalo, author of *Thinking Like An Entrepreneur* and owner of Hupalo, Ltd.

"Infuse your marketing strategy with honesty and respect, and you'll be rewarded with loyal, relationship-based customers that bring you continual—and increasing—profits."

Susan Carter, small business operations consultant and author of *How To Make Your Business Run Without You*

"A treat to find a book that has real substance to it....Teaches you how to increase your profits and create satisfied customers by working with your customers and your competition. I am already using many of its tools and techniques....Marketing as it should be done!"

Mark Frank, author of *Start Your Own Home-Based Website Design Business*

"A road map for ethical, effective and friendly marketing ... easy-to-read style."
Susan Sanders-Kinzel, Cumuli Ezine Finder

"Dismisses 'quick buck' marketing strategies and presents the real secret for succeeding in today's increasingly cynical marketplace ... trust, integrity and reciprocity."
Steven Van Yoder, author of *Get Slightly Famous*

"I can hardly wait to put "marketing ju-jitsu" and other tips into practice ... and I've never had that reaction to a marketing book! But the real value ... is its emphasis on an ecology of marketing and business, which can evolve in parallel with human society towards a non-predatory, sustainable way of life."
Laurel Lyon, Minisitetemplates.com

"PR Leads grew to a six-figure company in less than 12 months by following ethical marketing practices, working with competitors, and following the other valuable concepts outlined in this indispensable book."
Dan Janal, founder, PR Leads

"Everyone involved in marketing, sales, or customer relations needs to read this unique blueprint for ethical and rewarding business practices."
Lisa A. Smith, nonfiction editor and author of *Business E-Mail: How to Make It Professional and Effective*

"Cooperation, even with so-called competitors, can be beneficial for everyone to whom you come in contact."
Don Goddard, owner, Calm Spirit Oriental Medicine

"Our moms taught us to play fair. Now Shel tells ... us how to increase business, save time and money by dealing ethically with prospects, clients, and even competitors."
Virginia Lawrence, Ph.D., CogniText: Information Architecture

"Shel has managed to put onto paper, clearly and succinctly, marketing principles that I've been using successfully for many years. In addition, his book has shown me a number of new ideas which take ethical, customer-oriented marketing to new levels."
Keith Thirgood, creative director, Capstone Communications Group

"This is the book for those of us looking for hard data to support our intuition ... that yes, there is a better way to do business."
Susan Tull, Susan Tull Marketing Communications

"Filled with real life examples, his book provides Cliff Notes on the successful marketing methods of dozens of companies, condensed down to easy-to-read sections."
Patrick Kilhoffer, Directconnectionsint.com

Not only do you outline a more successful methodology for marketing and sales people, but you wrapped up excellent customer retention technique in the package. Having been in marketing for over two decades, I have to agree with you. The pie is not finite.... I also enjoyed the wealth of references to consumer surveys and comple-mentary business materials.... The marketing world needs more opinions like yours. Excellent work, as usual."

Linda Caroll, MultimediaJungle.com

"Convincingly shows that the real profit lies in treating your customers like the ab-solute gold they are.... Gives countless eye opening examples of ways you can easily increase your bottom line by doing the simplest things."

Ed Osworth, author and consultant, creator of the Internet Marketing Index

"Marketing requires looking at the glass as half full."

Karyn Zoldan, owner, Bridgemarketing.com

"You can win **and** your competitor can win. In fact, Shel shows you how, if you do it right, you can even turn your competitors into allies...challenges everything we thought we knew about marketing...always gives you more than you paid for, more than you expected."

Ned Barnett, APR, CEO, Barnett Marketing Communications, author of nine books on PR, advertising and marketing

"A course in marketing for mensches. Stop wallowing in the sleazy world of big busi-ness and learn how doing the right thing will actually improve your bottom line!"

Fern Reiss, author of *The Publishing Game*

"Needed by everyone that has or is thinking about starting a business. It means the difference between success or failure."

Lorenzo Rothery, Profitonthenet.com

"It may be hard for a rich man to get to heaven...but not impossible! When you operate with ethics and service, Shel shows you how to win friends, prosperity, **and** peace of mind!"

Joe Nicassio, Rapid Results Marketing

Principled Profit:

marketing
that
puts
people
first

SHEL HOROWITZ

AWM Books
Northampton, MA
A "People First" Book

Publisher's Cataloging-in-Publication Data

Horowitz, Shel

Principled profit : marketing that puts people first / Shel Horowitz.

p. cm.

Includes bibliographical references and index

ISBN 0-9614666-6-9 (alk. paper)

1. Marketing—Management

2. Business—Ethics

3. Business—Cooperative

HF5415.13 .H675 2003

Library of Congress Control Number: 2003090557

AWM Books

Division of Accurate Writing & More

PO Box 1164

Northampton MA 01061 USA

413-586-2388

http://www.principledprofit.com

http://www.frugalmarketing.com

http://www.frugalfun.com

http://www.accuratewriting.com

First Printing, June 2003

Printed in the United States

Acknowledgments

I want to thank (in alphabetical order within each category)...

- Those sources who kindly gave permission for me to quote large chunks of their material: Bob Burg, John Kremer, Amory Lovins, John Todd, Barbara Waugh.

- My wonderful wife, Dina Friedman, for her insightful critique of the first draft.

- Eric Anderson, Tom Antion, and Jeff Eisenberg, who pointed me toward additional research relevant to some of my examples.

- The vast number of people who helped me struggle through the two-month process of finding the right title and cover, including members of the Pub-Forum discussion list, subscribers to Shel Horowitz's Monthly Frugal Fun or Frugal Marketing Tips, participants in the Adventive discussion lists and others who just chimed in to help. Many, many people participated in the collaborative process of naming this book, and quite a few gave me more substantial help. Those I would like to name: Bradley Adams, Lyn Adelstein, Eric Anderson, Jason Anderson, Lorilyn Bailey, Lynne Bliss, Yvette Borcia (who wouldn't let me settle for a substandard choice), Martha Bullen, Laurie Burke, Steve Carlson, Alan Canton, Bobbi Chukran, Dawson Church, Linda Cirino, Rick Coates, Shannon Collins, Kimberly Converse, John Culleton, Jim Donovan, Stacey Fitzsimmons, Jacque Foreman, Sherry Fossum, Michel Fortin, Dina Friedman, Everett Gavel, Jeanne Gipp, Bob Goodman, Peter Goodman, Pam Gotcher, Lisa Grant, Jaimie Hall, Charles Hayes, Geoffrey Heard, Rick Herron, Andy Hockenbrock, Julie Hood, Jeff Hope, Alana Horowitz Friedman, Barbara Hubbard, Barbara Hudgins, J.J. Israel, Lee Jackson, Azriela Jaffe, Stephanie Jukes-Amer, Barry Kerrigan, Lynn Ketola, Theresa Klein, Paul Krupin, Wendy Kurtz, Diane Landi, Lynnette Lemke, Nanette Levin, Bobbi Lewis, Sandra Linley, Mayapriya Long, Reno Lovison, Robin MacRostie, Chris Marion, Bernard M. Markstein III, Robin Mayhall, Cort McCadden, Dorothy Molstad, Davina Morgan-Witts , Komra Moriko, Stephen Morris, Scott Morrison, James Nugent, Jill O'Neil, Charles Patterson, Jayne Pearl, Joan E. Phelps, Patsy Price, Kathy Rapp, Andrea Reynolds, John Richardson, Eva Rosenberg, Virginia Schulman, Jacqueline C. Simonds, Linda Singleton-Driscoll, Lisa Smith, Bob Spear, Cathi Stevenson, Judith Sulik, Stephen Taylor (who went above and beyond the call of duty), Lauren Teton, Nicole Vadnais, Ian Wade, Faith Waude, Barbara Waugh, Gayle Webert, Carol Welsh, Gloria G. Wolk, Gloria Yoshida, Leo B. Zaslov, Zachary Zucker. I'm sure I missed some people, and I apologize.

- The many generous people who gave me a blurb, or attempted to connect me with well-known "blurbers": Tom Antion, Linda Arellano, John Audette, Lorilyn

Bailey, Ned Barnett, Yvette Borcia, Sheldon Bowles, Walt Boyes, Ira Bryck, Bob Burg, Ellen Cagnassola, Jack Canfield, Linda Carroll, Susan Carter, Bobbi Chukran, Marisa D'Vari, Jim Dietz, Jim Douglass, Mona Doyle, Laura Ehrlich, Barbara Ellmore, Ken Evoy, Mark Frank, David Frey, Eric Gelb, Don Goddard, Jim Hightower, Anne Holland, Harry Hoover, Peter Hupalo, Azriela Jaffe, Dan Janal, Brian Jud, Patrick Kilhoffer, John Kremer, Jay Levinson, Laurel Lyon, Susan Z. Martin, Joe Nicassio, Denise O'Berry, B.L. Ochman, Ed Osworth, Jayne Pearl, Allan Pollet, Robert B. Reich, Fern Reiss, Melanie Rembrandt, Martha Retallick, Al Ries, Melanie Rigney, Eva Rosenberg, Lorenzo Rothery, Josh Samuels, Susan Sanders-Kinzel, Lisa Smith, Kristie Tamsevicius, Keith Thirgood, Debbie Thurman, Susan Tull, Steven Van Yoder, Mary Westheimer, Marsha Wilson, Gloria Wolk, Justin Worthley, Steve Yankee, Simon Young, Karyn Zoldan,

▓ My fabulous production team: Laurie Burke of Subtext Communications (interior design), John Culleton of Able Indexers and Typesetters (index), Robin MacRostie of ChoreoGraphic Design (interior illustration), Andrew Morris-Friedman (publicity photo), Virginia Schulman (copy editing), Brandy Toberman and the team at United Graphics (printing), Jamon Walker of Mythic Studio (cover design).

▓ Ed Ciriello, Claudia Gere of Claudia Gere & Co., and the entire membership of Pub-Forum and Self-Publishing, who connected me with important publishing resources.

To my parents...

my mother, Gloria Yoshida, whose strong social conscience helped me find my own; my father, Norman Horowitz, who taught me not only the value of a dollar, but that there are many things more important than money; and my stepfather, Michihiro Yoshida, a painter and writer who inspires me with his life-long quest for excellence in every endeavor.

Contents

xiv

part one
THE WAY OF THE GOLDEN RULE

"We don't function alone, but as members of a team."
Jay Conrad Levinson, author of the Guerrilla Marketing series of books[1]

Introduction

People *do* matter! This book shows you how to be a successful marketer while keeping your actions ethical. It's about the idea that you don't have to be crooked or mean-spirited to succeed in business. In fact, the success strategies of a business formed out of abundance and grounded in ethics and cooperation are powerful and long-lasting—and they help you feel good about yourself even while bringing in profits.

Your parents and teachers probably taught you to treat others the way you want to be treated, play fair, and cooperate. This book is about the idea that you can use those principles as a cornerstone of your business, and that you can design marketing that not only follows this precept, but harnesses its incredible power to bring success and abundance into your life.

Too many businesses see marketing as a weapon of war. They think that to succeed, they have to climb over their competitors, fool their customers, and herd their employees into constricted conformity. I think that's just plain wrong.

Marketing is a series of partnerships—of courtships, really. Businesses that succeed with my model understand that they have to woo their customers, just as a suitor woos for the chance to marry. And just as a successful marriage is built on years of mutual communication and meeting each other's needs, successful marketing looks for a deep and long-lasting relationship based on meeting the needs and wants of everyone involved. That means your customers, your employees, your suppliers, and, yes, even your competitors! You can knock someone's socks off on the first date, but if you betray that trust afterwards, you become your own biggest obstacle on the road to success.

1. Stated in a teleseminar he did for Radio TV Interview Report, Sept. 30, 2002. Used with permission.

So stay out of "marketing divorce court"; be there for the long term. It takes work to achieve a successful, long-lasting marriage, but the rewards are worth it. Similarly, you have to work at a successful long-term relationship with all the other interest groups that interact with your business. It's got to be something that works for everybody involved.

Just as a romance that's based on false promises and miscommunication is doomed to failure, so business relationships based on greed and backed by false promises aren't going to work over time. But the good news is that if you treat others well, they will become your best marketers. The better you treat others, the more they will want to do business with you.

A word on terms: There are many ways to express the concept of Marketing That Puts People First, and to keep the book interesting, I use many of them. In fact, I spent over a month searching for the perfect title for this book, and many of the terms came from the more than a hundred titles I considered and discarded. Whether I say "everyone wins," "mutual benefit marketing," "marketing from abundance," "cooperative marketing," "ethical, profitable marketing," or some other phrase, it all boils down to this: You make your own success by helping others succeed—you succeed without selling your soul. Think about this style of business as a practical, day-to-day expression of the old Golden Rule: Do unto others as you would like others to do unto you—a precept found in every major religion.[2]

Although I do believe very strongly in the Golden Rule, this is not a religious book. Rather, it's based on a code of ethics. Your ethics might or might not be religiously based; the important thing is that you have an ethical basis for your behavior, including your professional or business behavior.

The modern business world doesn't always assume that business should be based on ethics. But I do. I will assume that you're reading this book because you really want to do what's right; but perhaps you've been steeped in so many years of "Nice Guys Finish Last" that you aren't sure it's really possible to succeed, thrive, and be profitable while doing the right thing.

2.   Stephen Apatow of the UK-based Humanitarian Resource Institute, in his "The Golden Rule Principle: Global Religious Leaders Called to Re-Focus on This Universal Objective of the Interfaith Community," cites 13 examples from primary religious texts, from Buddhism to Zoroastrianism <http://www.wfdd.org.uk/Documents/IF/Golden_Rule_Principles.pdf?>. (All URLs in this book were live as of when I did my research. Although I cannot guarantee their continued availability, since they're not on my own sites, you can easily find similar data using Google.com or other search engines.)

I'm here to tell you that you *can* succeed and still keep your conscience. In this book, you'll encounter many success stories that put a practical handle on this philosophy. You'll see that others are doing very well by doing good, and that you can too.

1

Basic Concepts

The Road to Your Success: Providing Value to Others

In the business world, we hear a lot about cutthroat competition and gaining advantage over the enemy. In some circles, it seems to be a game to see how best to cheat your customers.

These are the concepts of win-lose marketing, and I believe this kind of thinking is a dinosaur; it won't survive.

This book is about Marketing That Puts People First. Most of the time, everyone can win—nobody has to lose. Not only can you succeed in business by doing the right thing with every person and business that interacts with you—but often, **it's the only way to succeed**.

Don't take my word for it—listen to some experts:

1. Consumers avoid buying from companies they perceive as unethical.

   A 1999 survey of consumers in 23 countries by Environics International, in cooperation with The Prince of Wales Business Leaders Forum and The Conference Board, found that 40 percent of consumers had considered punishing a company based on its social actions, and nearly 20 percent had actually avoided a company's products because of its social actions. A 1998 study commissioned by the UK-based Cooperative Wholesale Services found that 60 percent of retail food customers, even in the absence of an organized boycott, have avoided a shop or product they associated with unethical behavior.[3]

2. Consumers prefer to buy from companies that support their social agenda.

   A 1997 study by Walker Research found that when price and quality are

3. Business for Social Responsibility's "Marketplace" White Paper, <http://www.bsr.org/BSRResources/WhitePaperDetail.cfm?DocumentID=269>. Downloaded Jan. 16, 2003.

equal, 76 percent of consumers would switch brands or retailers to a company associated with a good cause. Criteria frequently cited by consumers as affecting their purchasing decisions include environmental responsibility, community philanthropy, and avoiding the use of "sweatshop" or child labor.[4]

Many consumers also actively support companies that court business from their ethnic or subculture group. African-Americans control $320.6 billion in discretionary spending; Latino-Americans control $261.2 billion; people with disabilities, $176 billion.[5] Gay and lesbian purchasing power is about $400 billion.[6]

Another growing area of company interest is cause-related marketing, in which companies align with charities or causes in a marketing campaign. Such campaigns have become increasingly common as consumers become more accepting of the concept. For many companies, the question is no longer whether to participate in cause-related marketing, but which cause to embrace.[7]

3. Investors have shifted 13 percent of all investment dollars into socially responsible companies.

In November 1999, the Social Investment Forum reported that more than $2 trillion was invested in the United States in funds identified as socially responsible, an increase of 82 percent from 1997 levels. This represents roughly 13 percent of the $16.3 trillion under professional management in the US, or one out of every eight dollars.[8]

It's a radical new way of looking at the world.

Spend an hour or two with this book, and you may find that you no longer live in a dog-eat-dog world—and that in fact, when the dogs learn to work together, they can accomplish much more than any of them could on their own. Think of the incredible weight a team of sled dogs can comfortably pull across the snow; no one dog could accomplish that. And thus, when you join forces with others—even those you've been trained to think of as your competitors—truly amazing things can happen.

4. Ibid.
5. Ibid.
6. "The Gay and Lesbian Market Today," Howard Buford, president, Prime Access, Inc., 2001 <http://www.multiculturalmarketingresources.com/experts/art_gaylesbian.html>.
7. Business for Social Responsibility's "Marketplace" White Paper, op. cit. in fn. 3.
8. Ibid.

This is an opinionated and personal book; I make no pretense otherwise. It is based on my own experience of over 25 years in marketing. I've used the principles in this book, and the practical ideas in my earlier book, *Grassroots Marketing: Getting Noticed in a Noisy World*, to build a successful, independent business that is over 20 years old. I want you to do at least as well.

Why Is This Approach Better?

Compare these scenarios:

1. The doctor says your ulcer is a little better, but you're still overdoing it. You put in 65-hour weeks and you still can't get everything done—but your family life is suffering and your stress level is high. So much of your time is spent cold-calling people who don't even want to talk to you, let alone buy from you. And your best sales manager just got stolen away by your biggest competitor, taking a client list and inside knowledge about your company's business strategy.

2. You're enjoying a quick, relaxing weekend getaway with your family; it's a celebration of the big new client you landed. You got the contract because a previous happy customer, a competitor of your new client's, recommended you. That makes sense, because your customer has been so pleased at the way your services generated profits that she can't help spreading your name around. You also think back on the industry conference at which you spoke recently, and how, coming out of that event, your firm is joining with three others to form a strategic alliance that will build all of your businesses. Life is good, and you're glad to spend this time with your spouse and children. Only a few years ago, it seems that you never had any time to spend with them, that you were spinning like a hamster on an exercise wheel—always working but never getting ahead. How glad you are that you've found a better way!

In the pages that follow, you'll learn how to begin setting a course for the smooth channel of success, instead of the rocky shoals of stress. And you will achieve this by helping others meet—or surpass—their goals.

The Magic Triangle: Quality, Integrity, Honesty

Ready for the big principle of this book? It's not a secret at all, just a simple truth. But it's crucial. Here it is:

Create value for others in everything that you do

That's the "magic formula"! You help yourself best when you're helping others. And the way you do that is by basing your business on a solid foundation of three principles:

Quality, Integrity, Honesty

Quality: Provide the best value you can.

Integrity: Run your business in alignment with your core values; don't try to be something you're not.

Honesty: Value the truth and be eager to share it with your prospects and customers—even if it means that your solution is not the best for them right now—in other words, it may not be appropriate for a particular prospect to become a customer at this time.

I make a big part of my living writing marketing materials for other businesses. Because I try to deliver extremely high quality while keeping my prices affordable, the value of my work to my clients is very high—and my customers become my "marketing evangelists" because they're excited and delighted by the impact my work has on their business. Integrity keeps me close to my core values. Those include making the world a better place, having work that I find meaningful, and enjoying a high quality of life. Out of honesty, I've turned down work projects because another person might be better equipped to do the job; out of integrity, I've refused work assignments that clashed with my values.

You may be surprised to find out that becoming super-rich is *not* one of my goals. In fact, it's integral to my value system to show ways of having a truly high-quality life, one filled with joy in the form of travel, music, good food, and more—and to show that this can be done while living lightly and spending lightly. (In fact, my first website, <http://www.frugalfun.com>, is dedicated to this idea.) I work because I enjoy what I do—I take great satisfaction in writing and speaking, and in knowing that I do these things quite well—and I believe that the world becomes a better and more interesting place if I can create excitement in a book by an unknown author or explain to the world how to have fabulous vacations that don't cost much.

As for honesty—it not only feels like the right thing, it's also good for business. For instance, my books on how to save money on marketing cover much of the same ground. When someone orders both books, I always explain that one of the books is all they need—and which one, and why. People are invariably shocked that I actually tell my customers that they should reduce the amount of my sale. But I want a long-term customer relationship—and word-of-mouth buzz—more than the short-sighted short-term profit of selling customers a book they don't need.

Who Wins When You Market with Quality, Integrity, and Honesty?

Usually, everybody. Your customers or clients realize you're not trying to cheat them. And they will so value the experience of being treated well that they will come back again and again. They even tell others.

Your suppliers will relate to your honesty and integrity, to the knowledge that you understand that they and you are partners who can both go farther by helping each other.

Your competitors benefit, too, especially if they see that your ethical behavior opens the way for them to improve their own operating standards. As you make space in the market for quality, integrity, and honesty, you begin to see each other less as rivals and more as people who can work together to make things better. And we'll see a little later that with this cooperative model, you can help each other in many ways.

2

Marketing Versus Adversarial Sales

Marketing Instead of Sales

Recently, I went to New York to speak as part of a panel of six people discussing sales and marketing for solo entrepreneurs. One of my copanelists was a "Sales Jerk" who monopolized about 70 percent of the panel's time; he was thoroughly aggressive, rude, and arrogant. His advice to others was that they, too, should be aggressive. He went on and on about how you just have to pick up the phone and cold call, hour after hour, day after day. His theory seemed to be that if you were a thorn in the side of enough people, one or two of them would do business with you, just to get rid of you.

You probably won't be surprised that I disagree, strongly. With his approach, everyone loses. He's going to have to work 14 hours a day at alienating people, in order to make a decent living. He's wasting a lot of effort that could be spent far more productively, and he's destroying the chance to build the long-lasting, positive relationships that turn prospects into customers voluntarily. What sales he gets will be in spite of his approach, not because of it—but eventually the numbers do add up to a livable income. My guess is that he could sell a lot more and work a lot less if he followed the sales methods I discuss in this book.

When I finally got a chance to say a few words, I said, "Now, here's the difference between marketing and sales. I never make cold calls. I create marketing that has the prospect calling me! When I get the phone call or the e-mail, they're already convinced that I can help them. If I don't screw it up, I have the account." While this may be an oversimplification—sometimes, I'm on the "short list" of three or four vendors, rather than automatically chosen as the preferred vendor—it is actually the dominant marketing trend in my business.

We were the last panel of the day; a cocktail reception followed. For the entire two hours of the reception, people came up to me, thanked me for what I'd said, and told me they thought the other guy was a jerk! Many asked for business cards or thumbed through my book. Some have since approached me about becoming clients.

Is my approach successful? Judging by how challenging it's been to carve out the time to write this book amid all my client projects, I'd have to say that it is quite successful. I spend a lot of time on marketing, and virtually none on the actual sales process, until a prospect contacts me (or contacts a discussion list where I'm active, and expresses a need that I can help with). Then, I either discuss over the phone how I can help meet the needs they have, or send a quick prewritten e-mail with a few lines of personalized response at the beginning. And here's the best part—when someone does contact me, my close rate for marketing services is about 80 percent.

Of course, this success did not happen overnight. I have worked at it long and hard, and each time I've moved my business to a new service sector, I've had to build up my client base and make a very gradual transition toward serving that type of client. But I now have quite a number of clients who have been coming to me for several years—they always have nice things to say about my work when others ask, and occasionally initiate entirely new income streams for me by asking if I'm able to provide a new service.

Back to the "Sales Jerk" and his selling style, for a minute. Here is another key principle of ethical, profitable marketing:

Conduct your business so as to build long-term loyalty

When you get a customer, you want to keep that customer and build a sales relationship that can not only last years, but also create a stream of referral business. When you select and hire an employee, you want that person to stick around so that you get the benefit of the time and trouble you invest in the initial training, and in the skills that employee develops as he or she works a few years in the position. When you select a supplier, you'd rather not have to go through the decision process and evaluate all the competitors again. And when you put time and energy into a joint venture, you'd generally like that cultivated relationship and hard work to result in long-term mutual success.

It is almost always much cheaper—and more profitable—to bring an existing customer back to purchase again than to prospect for and develop a new customer. Nortel cited a study showing that, "a mere 5 percent increase in customer retention can translate to as much as a 75 percent increase in profitability."[9] In a similar vein, ZD Net reported on a Gartner Group finding that "it costs five times as much to find a new customer as it does to keep an old one....Gartner estimates the cost of customer acquisition to be $280 a head, versus a mere $57 a head for customer retention." [10]

If these dollar figures are accurate, that would mean that if you're selling something in the $100 range, you are probably barely breaking even on purchases by your existing customers (subtracting not only the marketing cost but the actual production or wholesale cost of the item), and losing substantial amounts of money on every sale to a new customer. However, using more frugal strategies—which I discuss in *Grassroots Marketing: Getting Noticed in a Noisy World* and on the Frugal Marketing website—it ought to be easy to bring down the dollar costs substantially for both new-customer acquisition and retention. In my business, the largest amount I pay to acquire a customer, other than when colleagues refer clients and receive a commission on the first order, is for those who find me in the Yellow Pages—and that generally works out to less than $11. But more and more of my clients find me in other, cheaper ways, most of which cost only my time. Since my primary customer-retention strategy is to deliver superior work, at an affordable price, and within a reasonable time, my cost to keep an existing client is close to zero.

A more broad-based study by Howard Seibel, for E-Metrics, showed new-customer acquisition costs ranging from $8.66 for online travel discounter PriceLine all the way up to $700 for a mortgage origination firm. Most of the study's examples ranged between $14 and $300.[11] Even more extreme,

9. Cited in a Nortel sales document <http://www.nortelnetworks.com/network/retention.html>.
10. "CRM: Pay Attention to Retention," Adrian Mello, ZDNet, Aug. 22, 2002 <http://www.zdnetindia.com/biztech/ebusiness/crm/stories/64691.html>.
11. "Overview of Customer Acquisition Costs," Howard Seibel, managing director of Wharton Strategic Services, Target Marketing of Santa Barbara's E-Metrics, July 5, 2002 <http://www.targetingemetrics.com/articles/acquisition.shtml>

Harry Tennant and Associates found that Amazon.com had dropped cus-tomer-acquisition cost to $7 by the fall of 2000,[12] while the August 1, 2002 issue of *Ward's Dealer Business* (an auto-industry trade magazine) cites a new-customer acquisition cost for car dealers of $1000.[13]

The dollar costs may be overstated in the Gartner study, but the ratio still holds. For some firms, it may be low; I'd heard for years that the average cost of acquiring a new customer was around seven times the cost of retaining an existing customer. Still, recent savings through better databasing and online marketing have reduced marketing costs, so figures of four to five times are now typical.[14]

And how do you retain existing customers? By providing a pleasant, high-quality experience during the buying process; by offering goods and services that offer genuine value to the customer; and by exceeding your own promises and your customer's expectations—*not* by making enemies of your customer during or after the sales process!

Now, we begin to see the true short-sightedness of the "Sales Jerk" ap-proach. When people buy in spite of your sales style and not because of it, there is virtually no chance for a long-term sales relationship. You've gone for the "quick hit," and it will come back to bite you. By failing to deliver a positive experience to the customer, you've pretty much ensured that he or she will go elsewhere...and tell friends and colleagues to do the same.

So, if this is true, why, *why*, WHY, do so many businesses stuff their heads firmly into the sand and create marketing "strategies" that can only antagonize their prospects? Consider these, among many other examples of doing it all wrong:

- Dishonest "bait-and-switch" tactics in the showroom
- Obnoxious, unwanted—and untargeted—telemarketing
- Annoying saturation ad campaigns in electronic media
- In-your-face, unpleasantly loud tradeshow presentations

12. "What's Wrong with the Net?" Harry Tennant, Harry Tennant and Associates, Mar. 25, 2001 <http://www.htennant.com/hta/askus/wrong.htm>.
13. "Dealership Group Tests the CRM Waters...Cautiously," Cliff Banks, *Ward's Dealer Business*, Aug. 1, 2002 <http://wdb.wardsauto.com/ar/auto_dealership_group_tests/>.
14. See, for instance, "How to Recognize Value from Your Website Investment: Increasing the Lifetime Value of Customers through Process Automation," Intelygis.com White Paper pre-pared by Kilo Communications, Nov. 27, 2000 <http://www.intelygis.com/Resources/content/in_whitepaper.pdf>.

- A "don't bother me, I'm talking on the phone to my best friend" attitude from retail clerks
- Salespeople who can't listen or answer questions, and instead only spout their standard speech—whether or not it's appropriate or relevant
- Spam—junk e-mail—where the marketer claims permission was granted to a "marketing partner" (if this is true, why do I get so many addressed to long-defunct autoresponders?)

Let's take spam as an example, because it's easy to find commentary about it. Here's an acquaintance of mine, a successful Internet marketer, Paul Myers of <http://www.talkbiz.com>, complaining bitterly about the invasion of his e-box by so-called permission marketers who never got valid permission to make the contact:

Myers goes on at some length, attacking the tendency to add names to e-mail lists without explicit advance permission, and the all-too-frequent claim that it actually was requested—a claim rendered very dubious when the e-mail goes to an inbound-only address.

He concludes:

> Building a truly responsive list of targeted buyers isn't hard. It requires nothing more than offering solutions to problems that people care about, and telling the truth.
>
> People buy based on the relationship they feel with the listowner. A relationship started in dishonesty and fostered by the belief that the subscriber has the intelligence of a week old pizza isn't conducive to sales.[15]

Let's hear that last sentence again, Paul:

A relationship started in dishonesty...isn't conducive to sales

Paul is one of many, many people saying things like that—because they are true! To get long-term positive sales relationships, treat your customers as intelligent people, as partners in your business. Marketing strategies that insult your customers' intelligence are a foolish waste of money because even if you get a one-shot sale, you haven't built that relationship. In fact, you've pretty well forced the people you duped to go elsewhere the next

---

15. *I-Sales Digest*, Sept. 27, 2002, quoted with the writer's permission. *I-Sales* is one of several excellent newsletters available from Adventive; see Resources section.

time, and that means you have to go out and expensively acquire another customer.

And again, this is true in any marketing medium, not just e-mail. I remember an ad in my local paper, years ago, with the headline: "Sex"

Underneath it, "Now that I've got your attention…"

Were this an ad for condoms, pregnancy counseling, treatment of sexually transmitted diseases, or one of a dozen other things, it might have been an appropriate strategy.

But—it was an ad for a car dealership! In spite of the sexy models car makers use to sell their product, buying a car has nothing to do with sex. The attention that the ad got was entirely wasted. In fact, it was negative. I imagine that I was not the only person who crossed that dealership off the list of possible places to buy a car, because anyone who would insult my intelligence with that ad was not a company I'd do business with.

And then there was the salesman who came to my house with an appointment and wasted an hour or more of my time and my wife's time for a presentation that should have taken 15 minutes. Time is extremely precious to us. I actually needed what he was selling, but his unwillingness to deviate from his prepared speech did not work. This would have been a fairly easy sale if he had been able to listen to what we were saying, answer the questions we asked instead of the ones asked by the hypothetical prospect in his presentation, and cut to the chase instead of forcing us through the entire thing. He ignored repeated explicit requests to move faster. Only because we genuinely—desperately, in fact—needed the product and did not know of alternatives did we make it through until the end.

I will be honest: we were a lot younger and less sophisticated, we did not have access to the Internet for competitive research, and he actually did close the sale. But I wrote a letter to his supervisor saying that he got the sale in spite of his presentation and not because of it, and asking for a different rep to actually service the account—not the sort of thing you want in your employee file! And when our year's contract was up, we went with a different company, and stayed with the new provider for many years.

Telemarketing is usually done all wrong, too. It's gotten to the point where unless we already have a relationship with the company, we won't even listen. If the product is something we might have an interest in, we ask for materials in writing (and it's amazing how few of these salespeople actually follow up). If we have no interest, we politely and quickly ask to be placed on the Do Not Call list, and we hang up. Yet some of these cretins actually call back and try again!

This is not a strategy for long-term success. One of the things they ought to teach in basic sales training is to approach the prospect the way the prospect wants to be approached. If I say that I like things in writing and the salesperson can't be bothered to mail or fax me some information, why should I consent to a time-wasting sales call—to say nothing of an in-person appointment—just because that's the way the company would prefer to sell to me? Is it any wonder that society has such scorn for salespeople?

But Wait—It Gets Worse!

It wouldn't be so bad if win-lose marketers only shot *themselves* in the foot. Unfortunately, as soon as someone invents a new communication tool, somebody else figures out a way to abuse it.

E-mail is a classic example. E-mail at its best—in the form of discussion groups—may be the single most powerful marketing tool invented to date. It allows instant communication, anywhere around the world, with many thousands of people on a discussion list talking about the exact subject where you offer solutions—as easily as you can send a note to your next-door neighbor.

It also allows something very close to real-time dialog with individual correspondents thousands of miles away. And of course, you can back up statements with spreadsheets, research sources, articles, and other data, either as file attachments or posted on a Web page. For most users, in the US at least, it costs nothing extra to take advantage of these tools. (Many people in other parts of the world pay based on time online or bandwidth, so for them, the flat-fee monthly pricing we enjoy may not be an option—and that's important information if you're in the habit of sending large files around.)

To a skilled marketer, e-mail was, until fairly recently, "the goose that lays the golden egg." But the abusers—spammers, con artists, scumware/spyware/virus programmers—are killing the golden goose. Consider this:

▪ Many users have filters that sort any unfamiliar e-mail addresses directly into the trash can

- Some corporations use e-mail systems that automatically strip out attachments

- Even if the recipient is hand-filtering, most e-boxes are so clogged with junk mail that it's easy to accidentally delete a legitimate message

- Delivery reliability has dropped due to overloaded infrastructure

- Some popular services, including AOL, Yahoo, and Hotmail, simply can't process the volume, and the recipient's e-mail system breaks down or is shut off for quota violation

- Enormous numbers of e-mail addresses go stale every year

For people who need to be accessible by e-mail—journalists, technical support people, and consultants who have an Internet-oriented clientele—this flood of bad mail becomes a huge burden. There have been a number of times when I opened an e-mail thinking it was probably junk, because of a poorly chosen subject line, and it turned out to be an inquiry from a client or book purchaser—I have to check! And occasionally I have accidentally trashed an important e-mail. I do use technological filters, although I scan the contents by eye before deleting. And I deeply resent the time sorting the junk takes out of my workday.

And of course, we put up the same kinds of mental or technological filters against postal junk mail, telemarketers, junk faxes (illegal for years, but it doesn't seem to matter), and the barrage of ads that keep upping the ante—ads in toilet stalls, for goodness sake! Is there no sanctuary anywhere from bad marketing?

So now you know the truth: Part of why I'm so zealous about the mutual benefit approach is that the win-lose people make it much harder for the rest of us. I'm selfish that way—if I can convince a few people to change their ways, I'll have made the world a better place. And that's something I like to do.

3
Sales the Right Way

Does the last chapter mean there's no place for salespeople any more? Not at all—but it does mean that some businesses don't need a sales force if their marketing is properly effective, and it also means that successful sales people will pursue a People First approach.

If you're going to do sales, start with sales consultant Jacques Werth's concept of High-Probability Selling: Figure out who really has a lot to gain by doing business with you, and approach those people—*only* those people.[16] But don't approach them with "I have something to sell you"; come to them from the point of view that *you're their ally.* They have a problem that you can help them solve, or you have something that will free up their resources (time, money, employee productivity, etc.). If the cost of not acting is seen as higher than the cost of taking action, you're very likely to make the sale. And not only that, but once you've begun working from that understanding, your customers will not even consider going else-where. Why should they bother choosing from other suppliers when you've already demonstrated your sincere and competent commitment to help them solve a pressing problem or use resources more effectively? Remember my response to the "Sales Jerk": the best marketing has the *customer* decide that you are the right person for the job. Your own customers and prospects can even become evangelists for you, and—if you ask politely—will give you referrals, or even introduce you to others.

Three Wise Sales Strategies from the UMass Family Business Center

It has been my good fortune to be the conference reporter for the UMass Family Business Center, which has had a number of programs on sales and

16. A book written by Werth and Nicholas E. Ruben, *High Probability Selling*, is listed in the Re-sources section.

customer service over the years. These are programs aimed at businesses very different from my home-based service business: manufacturers, retail stores, hotels, and funeral parlors, among others. Just so you don't think that I'm writing only from my own experience, or that these principles would only apply to a business similar to mine, I'd like to share some insights from a few of these seminars (please see the footnotes for Web links to the full articles).

Mike O'Horo, of Sales Results, Inc., suggests an approach similar to Jacques Werth's: "Get permission from people who already want your product—and change the sales focus from an unwanted intrusion to a welcome—and rewarded—provision of service."

Create a profile of your best current buyers—then look for prospects who match that profile. When you find them, don't pitch! Identify the "demand trigger": the problem your prospect urgently needs solved. Investigate collaboratively: ask questions and listen. Only switch to solution mode if the *prospect* decides to take action. Once buyers conclude that you offer four or five times greater value than the perceived risk, they feel *compelled* to buy.

Don't focus on product features, or even on generic benefits; stick to your client's specific and deep needs. Avoid the trap of pushing product; don't be "the most expensive human catalog." O'Horo says the buyer cares only about how you can improve three factors: the effect the client desires, the relationship between value and investment, and self-interest/ego needs.

Independent of your offer, ask deep, probing questions:

- "What is the biggest problem you face?"
- "How important is this problem?"
- "What positive effects would you expect if you fixed it—and what benefit would that have for your business?"
- "How does the problem affect you personally?"

Once you've asked, "shut up and listen." From the buyer's answers, you'll both recognize whether the issue actually needs attention—then let the *client* conclude that the cost of inaction is too high.

Explore why the problem hasn't been solved; ask, "What are the barriers to solving this problem?" Then determine how many others are affected. Ask, "Who beside yourself is the natural champion to lead the charge within your company?" Those people become natural allies in the selling process, too; they are sponsors or champions.

When you get positive responses to these sorts of questions, you've been given permission to sell together. As soon as you switch to telling, you've blown your credibility. If you're cross-selling outside your own expertise, bring in your resident expert: "Would you find it helpful to talk with someone who has solved this problem for many others?"

But you still need to differentiate your product from the competition—to show where you add the value. Show how you're different (*not* better; don't make the client feel stupid about an existing choice). If you've set the sales process up along O'Horo's principles, the client often won't even consider anyone else's solution; you've earned the right to advance to each successive next step.[17]

According to Susan Bellows, a sales trainer who uses David Sandler's Neuro-Linguistic Programming (NLP)–based sales methods, the chances of closing a sale are only 1 percent on a cold call, 50 percent on a call with a referral, and 80 percent or better on a personal introduction. So getting those referrals and introductions—right after they've bought from you is the best time, she says—will be a major shortcut to a successful sales career.[18] And of course, your chances of getting referrals and introductions are far greater with methods that respect and value your clients and prospects.

For Alexander Hiam, author of *The Portable MBA* and many other books, the most important aspect of customer retention is providing a high-quality experience to the customer. That means not only an excellent product, but also extreme emphasis on customer relationships—to the point where employees actually anticipate a customer's needs, and propose accurate solutions to problems the customer may experience, but hasn't yet articulated.

For instance, if you sell photocopiers with a five-year lifespan, don't wait until the customers start to complain in the fifth year about high repair costs. After four years, send a mailing to your customers, noting that their

17. "A Sales Trainer Who Guarantees 'Bulletproof' Results," *Related Matters*, UMass Family Business Center, Fall 2001, p. 3. The complete article is available at <http://www.umass.edu/fambiz/bulletproof_selling.htm>.

18. "Creating a Sales Revolution," *Related Matters*, UMass Family Business Center, Spring 1999, p. 7. The complete article is available at <http://www.umass.edu/fambiz/creating_sales_revolution.htm>.

machines are aging—and you want them to know about your "borrow-a-photocopier" plan, in which they can sign up to use a brand-new loaner while their own machine is down for repairs.

Instead of angry customers, frustrated that the equipment is down, you've created loyalists who are aware that you'll go the extra mile, alerting your customers to an issue that hasn't even surfaced yet, and providing an easy solution. Better still, there's a good likelihood that they'll like the modern machine so much better, they'll purchase one.

But this attention to the customer's overall experience has to be genuine; run the business the way you want to live. Relationships among family members (in and out of the business), employees, and customers are interrelated. Thus, the way you treat employees or family members will be reflected in the ways they treat your customers. Employees who are valued, who are asked to contribute to the thinking behind a business, will be more likely to make that extra push so that the client feels the specialness of his or her own relationship with the firm.

Hiam cited a wildly successful company, Rosenbluth International—one of the leaders in the corporate travel market. This firm gets $3 million in new business every day, and is growing at 15 percent a year. They do almost no traditional marketing, with an advertising-to-sales ratio of 0.00004. But in an industry where a 75 percent retention rate is considered terrific, this company retains 96 percent of its 1500 corporate clients. Rosenbluth will go so far as to open a new branch office, just to serve a new account.

Says Hiam, "Build relationships, never lose a customer. You grow with your customers," so that a company that spends $1000 on you in the early stages may spend $100,000 ten years later.

When there is a customer service issue, make sure your employees' language is in harmony with the results you want to achieve. If the goal is to have a happy customer, it's not enough to simply address the customer's grievance. Use language that accepts responsibility and moves the customer's agenda forward. For instance, instead of responding in a sentence that begins, "We would…," take personal responsibility for the outcome by starting your answer, "I will…" By using the more immediate, direct language, you communicate to the aggrieved customer that you have accepted the challenge to make it right. "I" can't be brushed off on anyone else. And "will" expresses a commitment to take action. "We would" simply doesn't have this power.[19]

When to Say No to a Sale

Let's turn for a moment from the idea of *selling* to the idea of *not selling*. When ethics are a major consideration in marketing, there will be times when you have to turn down work. One of the challenges, at least at first, is getting comfortable with the idea—especially challenging if you're a small entrepreneur just getting started, and you're used to struggling hard for every last dollar.

When would you need to refuse an order? Here are several situations, and they all come back to those three key attributes:

- You don't have the appropriate solution; someone else is better equipped to solve the client's problem (honesty)
- There isn't enough time to do the job well (quality)
- You could do the job, but it's an area you're trying to get away from (honesty—to yourself)
- The client will obviously be so high-maintenance and/or so demanding that the job isn't worth the price you can charge (quality—of the client)
- The client asks you to engage in unethical behavior (integrity)
- The product is too shoddy and you don't feel good about working on it (integrity/quality)
- You find the job itself morally distasteful (integrity)

As an example of that last bullet, I was developing a relationship with a local PR firm that wanted to subcontract some copywriting assignments to me. The very first job I got was so clearly wrapped up in a cause that I have spent my life working against that it actually made me ill to look at the client's publicity fliers. My only hesitation was knowing that the PR shop was overextended and needed materials on a short deadline; I didn't want to strand the woman who was subcontracting to me.

But after spending an hour agonizing about it, I picked up the phone and explained that while I didn't want to leave her hanging, I couldn't in good conscience take the job—but I could still help her manage her overload by taking on a different client.

---

19. *Related Matters*, UMass Family Business Center, Fall 1998, p. 7. The complete article is available at <http://www.umass.edu/fambiz/marketing_family_business.htm>.

I was fully expecting that she'd be furious—but actually, she told me she respected my stance. She did take back the problem assignment and give me one that I felt totally comfortable handling.

As a marketer, I used to take on projects for clients even if I didn't feel their products were good enough—but I've stopped. I discovered that if I think the product is shoddy, or a terrible value, or just unable to capture my interest, I can't write decent copy for it anyway. The last time I tried was a few years ago, when I was hired to write a press release for a truly trashy book on dating, with only a few words on each page and an absurdly high price for the value received. I did write the press release, but not only did I hate working on it, but the client hated what I turned in. From that point on, I decided that I would have to feel good about the product in order to take on the job.

I find that people respect me for this stance, and that I feel a lot better about the work I do. My conclusion? I should have started that policy years ago! Now, when a client contacts me about doing some work, there's a clause in my return e-mail that allows me the right to back out of a project if I don't feel it's a good fit.

Interestingly enough, Arthur Andersen the person, the founder of the accounting firm that was driven out of business by its willingness to look the other way when major audit flags kept turning up at Enron, lost a major account after refusing the company's request to engage in exactly the sort of unethical accounting that brought down his company almost 70 years later—at a very early stage in his career, when he wasn't sure he could meet his next payroll. He told the company president that there was "not enough money in the city of Chicago" to change his mind.[20]

---

20. This story is widely quoted; see, for instance, the *Chicago Tribune* of September 1, 2002 <http://www.chicagotribune.com/business/showcase/chi-0209010315sep01.story>. I first found it in a book called *Reclaiming the Ethical High Ground*, by John Di Frances (Wales, WI: Reliance Books, 2002).

4

Expand the Model Exponentially – By Making It Personal

Sales clearly lends itself very well to a People First strategy—especially since so many companies are completely clueless about how to achieve their own goals by working collaboratively to meet the prospect's goals. But sales is only one among many marketing tools. Now let's look at how everyone can win when marketing through the media.

Media publicity is free, and is valued more highly than advertising because it conveys the endorsement of a respected third party: the journalist.

The trick to getting media coverage is to remember that the journalist does not care about you or your business; the journalist cares about the story that readers, listeners, or viewers will find so important that they select that story from all the competing stimuli and choices, and allow the journalist to tell the story for them, in words and images.

John Kremer and Biological Marketing

Listen to an expert in working the media: John Kremer, author of *1001 Ways to Market Your Books* and one of the foremost authorities on book marketing in the US, recently spoke at a conference where I was also on the program. Although he directed his remarks at authors, publishers, and book marketers, his wisdom applies to anyone marketing anything: a product, a service, an idea, an attitude.[21]

> All marketing is essentially creating relationships: with press, distributors, printer, stores—the people who are helping your book get into the marketplace—and ultimately with

---

21. The next four excerpts are from his speech at the 3rd Annual Infinity Publishing "Express Yourself" Conference, Valley Forge, PA, October 3, 2002.

your readers, who are going to create the word-of-mouth army that will sell your book. What marketing ultimately is, is making friends. All business success is determined by how good you are at creating and maintaining relationships—in any field.

Of course, coverage in the media helps you to build those vendor relationships throughout the distribution chain, as well as to create demand from the ultimate customer. When you think of marketing as making friends, Kremer points out, it changes the way you market to the media, as well as to consumers.

Make a database of 100 key media contacts who really need to know about your book. You'll get more sales by focusing on relationships with these 100 key people.

99 percent of all [effort to contact] media is wasted. If you send 1000 press releases and 10 pick it up, the rest is wasted. Ideally, you put most of your emphasis into the one percent that does pay off. And do the follow up. There are some amazing mousetraps out there that nobody's beating a door to. Those inventors believed Emerson [who said, "Build a better mousetrap, and the world will beat a path to your door"], but it doesn't work that way. You have to create the path and pave it, and put in a landing strip for a plane or two.

He went on to broaden the discussion well past media coverage and out to the end user. He believes that if you turn your customer into a participant, the customer will develop an emotional attachment to your products. So, for example, let your customers have a say in choosing among different packaging alternatives or product names. In his case, he let visitors to his website vote on which of two cover designs they preferred—and they overwhelmingly chose the one he liked less, so he followed their advice. There are also more subtle ways to get this feedback—for instance, "Get buy-in from votes on your website. Offer a choice of one free report with several different titles" containing the same information. If there's a clear preference, that helps you name your product.

John has developed a new paradigm called "biological marketing," and with his permission, I will share it with you:

> Farmers have incredible ROI [return on investment]. They plant one seed of corn and get back 900. Nature does not follow physics. Instead of an equal and opposite reaction, there's an incredible multifold giving back. It follows biological laws, and when you give and share, it comes back to you in abundance. Physics says that the ultimate end of the universe is entropy. Biology says the opposite, that everything multiplies and becomes incredibly rich and diverse. That's the law of life. Physics is the law of non-life. And it's the laws of life that determine marketing.
>
> When you understand that, you know it's OK to give. The authors [or business owners] who are generous with their time get it back, they build legions of fans. That kind of relationship makes marketing fun and successful. You cannot replace it with mechanical rules, but once you learn it and take it to heart, that becomes the basis for success in anything you do. If you treat people right, it comes back over and over again. If you build a network of relationships, it's only three degrees of separation. Another part of the law of nature is that you have to break out of your shell, just as birds and reptiles do. You can do it one person to one person."[22]

John is referring to the popular concept of "six degrees of separation"—the idea that by knowing people who know other people, you can reach anyone in the world within just six contacts (I'm not passing judgment on the merits of the concept here).

Bob Burg and Winning Without Intimidation

To finish this chapter, I want to tell you about a guy who has done more to improve my attitude than just about anybody.

His name is Bob Burg and I've never met him, but I've been subscrib-

22. John Kremer is also working on a book about this; if you'd like to be notified when it's available, please send him a note:
<a href="mailto:JohnKremer@bookmarket.com?subject=NotifyBioMarketingShel">
JohnKremer@bookmarket.com with the subject "NotifyBioMarketingShel"</a>.

ing to his weekly newsletter, "Winning Without Intimidation," for quite some time.

Here's the basic premise: When you're in a situation where you aren't getting your needs met, find the best way to de-escalate potential conflict *and* get the results you want! He calls this principle "positive persuasion" or "winning without intimidation," and he is a master at it. One of his books, *Endless Referrals*, applies this concept directly to sales. This book was published by McGraw Hill and sold over 100,000 copies. His self-published *Winning Without Intimidation* also sold about that many, so clearly, Bob takes his own principles seriously. (Typical business books sell fewer than 10,000 copies; typical self-published books are lucky to sell 2,000.)

In every week's issue, Bob provides another real-life example of how he does this (or how his readers do it).

A lot of times, now, when I'm in a situation where things could get heated, I take a deep breath and a step back, and I say to myself, "How would Bob handle this?" And guess what—not all the time but a lot of the time, I'm able to access that smarter part of my brain that can figure out what Bob would do, defuse the conflict, and achieve my goal. Recently, for instance, I needed to resolve a situation on one of my e-mail discussion lists that was building my frustration level past the point of comfort. In my "pre-Bob" days, I might have written a nasty public post to shame the offenders into better behavior. Instead, I wrote a polite private note asking the two offenders, as a personal favor, to change their behavior. The response from both was extremely positive.

Here's a little taste of Bob—one article from a recent issue of his newsletter, reprinted with his permission.

A LESSON FROM JUSTIN

By Bob Burg

A subscriber from South Africa, author (*Create Your Self*) and talk-show host Justin Cohen, wrote to share with us a recent personal story of "Winning Without Intimidation." Here it is in his own words:

"Bob, just wanted to tell you about a win that I had utilizing WWI principles. I recently bought an apartment. I later discovered the geyser (South African term for the hot water system) was broken. Although this falls under 'failure to disclose', the previous owner didn't want to pay for it. Initially the lawyer handling the sale bluntly told the sales agent he would not try to secure payment from the previous owner. That's where WWI comes in. I wrote him a letter. I said my knowledge of the law was incomplete so if it was not fair to grant my request I would 'really understand' but, if there was any way he could secure payment from the previous owner, I would 'really appreciate it'. All I asked was for half payment. He called back. This is what he said: 'The previous owner is a nightmare to deal with but because you're a nice guy I'm going to make sure they pay for the whole geyser.'

"Thanks, Bob."

That was great! Let's review the principles Justin so expertly utilized.

#1 He chose to "respond" instead of "react." He kept his cool and, instead of getting angry, simply asked himself the best way to handle the situation.

#2 He admitted not knowing the law, implying that the lawyer to whom he wrote was a man of expertise. Contrary to what most people think, this is *very* powerful. Don't try and fake it; instead, play into the ego of the other person and allow him to feel good about himself.

#3 He played upon the person's own feelings of "righteousness." By saying, "If it was not fair to grant my request..." Justin let him know that he was confident the man would do the right thing. Also very effective. Keep in mind that most people want to "be good" and "do the right thing."

#4 He let him know that he'd understand if it couldn't be done, but would "really appreciate" it if it could. This was an excellent paraphrase of what I call "The Eight Key Words," which are, "If you can't do it, I'll definitely understand" and the follow-up, "If you could, I'd certainly appreciate it."

These are about the most effective words you can ever use in the persuasion process, providing you've set the situation up correctly with politeness and patience, as did Justin.

#5 He offered to accept payment of just half the amount. Although not necessary, a very nice touch. He's giving before getting. Of course, in doing all of this, the lawyer saw that Justin was nice, polite, reasonable, fair, and just a really good guy. And he gave him everything he wanted! And, why not?

Great job, Justin; you are truly a positive persuader...and thank you for basically writing my column for me this week.[23]

Many issues of "Winning Without Intimidation" include an article about defusing personal conflict, and another article on how to use his strategies in a sales context. I have found it tremendously useful in softening the sometimes harsh way I approach people. As a native of New York City, raised in a loud, in-your-face culture, I've also found Bob's approach helpful in talking to people from a different, quieter cultural background—such as the New England Yankee farm community where I live. It's very helpful to remember that my "natural" style can scare people off.

23. Bob Burg, "Winning Without Intimidation," Vol. 3, No. 17, June 26, 2002. In the Resources section, you'll find an order link for his e-book, *Winning Without Intimidation*—a compilation of the newsletter's first couple of years.

5

The New Marketing Matrix

It's a common—but not always correct—principle in the marketing world that you need multiple impressions to move someone up the ladder from unaware, to aware, to prospect, to customer, to evangelist. Many marketers use the figure of seven impressions within 18 months (though, as the bombardment of ads increases, many would say that those seven impressions need to be much closer together, or that even seven isn't enough).

So, in the traditional view, the more you rain down messages upon the head of any particular individual, the more you push that person toward being first a prospect, and then a customer. This strategy leads to saturation advertising—the sort of thing that Coca-Cola or McDonald's calls a marketing strategy.

But theirs is a "strategy" that only works if you have essentially unlimited resources. They can afford to throw away millions of dollars in advertising in order to assure that everyone hears their marketing messages—because some percentage of people actually do respond to the constant bombardment. But you and I cannot afford to buy that kind of saturation, nor should we want to. It's so much better to figure out who are our real prospects, and talk to them as colleagues in a mutually beneficial partnership.

There is a certain amount of truth in the theory of repetition, but it's only part of the picture.

Under the right conditions, *even a single marketing message may be enough* to move someone from totally unaware to writing the check.

Here's my twist on the formula:

The effectiveness of your marketing depends on three variables:

■ The relevance of your message to an individual's wants and needs at that exact moment

■ The quality of the message—and that includes the perceived value of your offer, the sense of trust and reliability that you've built, and the perceived quality of the product or service, as well as the quality of the user's experience of your marketing message (which, in turn, is created by the interplay of your message's copy, visuals, audio, and/or usability)

■ The number of times this individual is exposed positively to your messages

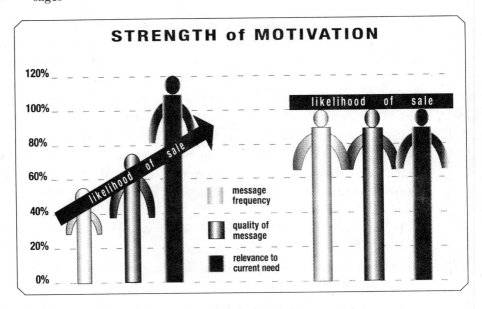

As you see, you are very likely to make the sale when all three of these variables are toward the top of the scale—but if any one variable is very high, a sale is quite possible even if the other variables are low. When they work in harmony or in sync, your chances are much greater. However, if one variable is strong enough, even if the others are weak, you can still close the sale (particularly if the strong one is relevance to current need).

In other words, if someone is looking for exactly what you offer, and you connect with that person through a beautifully crafted message that touches all his or her hot buttons, that person might be ready to buy immediately, on the first contact. And if the desire is strong enough, that person will take action, right then and there. If the desire is not yet strong enough, it may take several more messages—different messages, not an exact repeat—to convince your prospect to become a customer.

The frequency axis is particularly tricky. In general, more *unique* messages move the prospect forward toward making the purchase—in part because, over time, increased frequency artificially increases desire, so that eventually, the "need" to act on the desire moves up the ladder of the consumer's consciousness. However, repeating the exact same message in too close proximity will not be effective; it will start getting annoying very quickly. Think about watching a one-hour television show. If you hear the same commercial at the beginning and end of the show, you're likely to be pretty tolerant of it. But if you hear the same commercial at every single break, you might feel like throwing something at the TV after the third or fourth time it appears.

Yet if instead of the same commercial, the advertiser ran a series of six commercials, each of which stressed a different benefit, you'd probably still be listening by the end of the show, even if you felt the advertiser was overdoing it a bit.

Does that mean you should never repeat? No—just that you need to be careful. As I write this, a local college FM radio station is currently running a Public Service Announcement (PSA) about why they've stopped streaming their programming over the Web, how new rules have made it impossibly expensive, and a URL to visit to do something about it. As an occasional streaming audio listener, I am moved toward action by this PSA—but so far, I've only heard it twice in three weeks, and since both times have been in the car, I haven't had a chance to jot down the URL and make my visit. A greater frequency—say, once every couple of days—would probably be enough to burn that URL into my brain and get me to click over. (Of course, I could always call the station and ask, but so far, this spot hasn't motivated me to do that yet.) But the concept of the PSA—that I, as a user of the streaming service, have much to gain in creating pressure to change this new regulation—is definitely from the mutual-benefit book of strategies and tactics.

On the other hand, if the person is not a prospect, is not in the market for what you're selling, 20 messages will not move this person up the ladder.

To use the same example, if I had heard the spot back in the days when I connected to the Web over phone lines at 2400 bps, it wouldn't have mattered how often I heard the spot, I would never have been moved to action—because until I got broadband Internet, I was simply not a prospect for streaming audio.

Some would say that a marketer's job is to artificially create the desire—but I don't think that's following the Golden Rule.

If a consumer is already in the market—for a breakfast cereal, a car, a computer, whatever—it's totally appropriate to create interest in your particular product. But to push a consumer with no previous interest toward a product that doesn't address that consumer's real needs and wants is dishonest—and not conducive to that all-important long-term relationship.

So you win in marketing by reaching the exact people who are ready to buy—with a message they can't resist, because it appeals directly to their current wants and needs.

Think about it. Say, like me, you're moderately interested in new technology and how computers continue to make our lives easier. Right now, it's a mild, purely academic interest. Marketing messages about the latest technologies catch some small part of your attention and you file them deep in the back of your mind. Then suddenly you try to boot your computer and nothing happens; it's dead. Now, when you see an ad or an article about the latest technology, you pay very close attention. Since you need to replace the computer, you think carefully about which of those new capabilities or customer service qualities are important to you—and very quickly, you research the available choices and place an order. If a marketer happens to send you a mailing about a special sale on exactly the computer you need, you'll order it. But if you'd gotten the same mailing a week earlier, you'd have tossed it in the recycle bin.

The change in circumstances (your computer breakdown) moved you instantly three rungs up the ladder—from vaguely aware, right past prospect, and all the way up to *hot* customer, ready to move immediately.

Now the problem for marketers, of course, is knowing when that moment will happen—when changed circumstances convert someone from a non-prospect to a buyer—and how to be in the customer's mind at that magical moment, without having been a pest before the buyer made that transition. Here's where "pull media," such as Yellow Pages, classified ads, and the World Wide Web, can have a huge impact. Pull media are customer driven. They wait for a user to approach and "pull" the marketing information into their consciousness, unlike "push media," which thrust messages into the audience's awareness without being invited in. When the customer is finally ready and turns to such a medium, where he or she is in control of the selection process, then a previous build-up of positive, nonintrusive messages over time can provide immediate advantage to the savvy marketer.

A real-life example: In the spring of 2002, I had a kidney stone. Kidney stones cause extreme pain, and I remembered that a former participant on my publisher's discussion list had written a book about kidney stone treatment. I remembered that she had always been helpful and intelligent, not just about medical issues but about publishing topics as well.

I first tried entering her business name as a .com domain name; it didn't come up. So then I went to a search engine and searched for her business name plus the phrase "kidney stone." Instantly, I had her website and ordered the book. Because she had, over a period of years, established herself as the authority I would trust if I knew someone with a kidney stone problem, I didn't want or need to sort through all the results for kidney stone treatment; her prior participation had created confidence in me that she could give me the help I needed. Even though I used a pull medium, I had already chosen the vendor; only if I'd been unable to locate her would I have explored other options.

When I wrote the above, I hadn't come across other writing that pointed out the holes in the standard "rule of seven" (to use Jeffrey Lant's phrase). But as I was soliciting blurbs for this book, Jeffrey Eisenberg, of Future Now, Inc., pointed me toward Roy Williams's *Secret Formulas of the Wizard of Ads*. Williams refers to the "APE," or Advertising Performance Equation; the effectiveness of your advertising is directly tied to other variables beyond frequency, including the prospect's personal experience with the firm. He says that if you multiply your "Share of Voice"—the percentage of advertising in your category that comes from you—by the ad's power to convince ("Impact Quotient"), you get "Share of Mind," and then, when you multiply the result by the prospect's "Personal Experience Factor"—

direct experience of your company by the prospect—you can determine your market share. Multiply the Share of Market by the Market Potential (the number of customers actually out there) and you can determine your sales volume.

Expressed as a formula, it looks like this:

$$Sales\ Volume = SoV \times IQ \times PEF \times MPo$$

So customers who have positive previous experiences with a company are *far more likely* to respond to that company's ads than those with a history of bad experiences.[24]

I think Williams is on to something, but he misses one crucial point: advertising is only one part of marketing (often, the most expensive and least effective part). You can get to that share of mind and market without having to pay for it!

---

24. Roy Williams, *Secret Formulas of the Wizard of Ads*. (Austin: Wizard Academy Press, 1998), p. 47.

6
Abundance Versus Scarcity

The Old Scarcity Paradigm

The pie, you've always heard, is finite. If you win, someone else has to lose. There's not enough to go around. If you believe this, you're forced to spend lots of time and energy competing, striving to win and defeat the others.

But the whole premise of this book is that it's simply not true. There *is* enough to go around. Perhaps the distribution system needs some readjustment, but the pie keeps expanding. The eighteenth-century economist Malthus was wrong; the world produces enough for its growing population. And businesses can thrive and prosper without trying to drive their competitors out of business.

The "Prosperity Consciousness" Paradigm—and its Problems

A few years ago, it seemed all the buzz was about "prosperity consciousness"—about the idea that if you tapped into the right vein of the universe, you would be prosperous. Of course, with the stock market on a rapid-fire growth curve at the time, it seemed that prosperity was very easy to achieve. Then the stock market tanked, and all of a sudden nobody was talking about prosperity consciousness.

Being a bit of a marketing heretic, I had never put any store in the idea anyway. In fact, while all around me, I saw people talking about their great plans to achieve material wealth, I started writing about an alternative that made a lot more sense to me: "Abundance Consciousness."

Rather than working toward material wealth, I started counting the blessings in my life. And there were a great many!

■ Good health

- A family that loves me
- A beautiful house in the country with wonderful friends and neighbors
- Work that I truly enjoy—and that makes the world better
- Community involvements that also make the world better
- The chance to travel
- An average of six weeks of vacation per year
- A house full of books, art, and music
- Schools that stimulate my children's creativity
- Nearby colleges and cultural centers that bring amazing performances, exhibits, and lectures
- Closeness to nature, with terrific places to hike, bird-watch, bike ride, cross-country ski, and swim—either within walking distance or a very short drive away
- The pleasures of farm-fresh food and home-cooked gourmet meals, as well as the pleasures of sophisticated gourmet restaurant fare

And on and on it goes. My life is one of great fortune and privilege, but not one that revolves around material wealth. I've learned to be a good shopper for what I want, and I've discovered that I can live a very comfortable, dare I say pampered, lifestyle. It seems to me that many people I know who have a higher income are actually less happy than I am. They always seem to be desperate to go out and make more and more money, while I make a comfortable living but leave lots of time in my life to walk in the woods, explore foreign cities, enjoy family time, attend concerts, and so forth.

Although I didn't yet have the phrase, Abundance Consciousness, to express this idea, my early thinking on this topic was what inspired me to write my fourth book, *The Penny-Pinching Hedonist: How to Live Like Royalty with a Peasant's Pocketbook*. That book told every reader how to have more fun and spend less money doing it. I also was inspired to set up my first website, FrugalFun.com, back in 1996; it has grown to offer hundreds of articles that help people find abundance in their lives.

The New Vision: Not Scarcity, Not Prosperity, but Abundance

Here's another way to express that radical, heretical idea:

Your life can be abundant and full of blessings, with or without material wealth

The interesting thing is that when I opened my life up to that idea, it seemed to me that the already abundant blessings in my life increased.

Abundance is fundamentally different from prosperity. Prosperity still works on the idea that you have to win over others, that you have to strive for more money, and that the pie is finite; your gain is someone else's loss. Abundance says that there is enough to go around, even if there are some kinks in the distribution, and that helping others is one way to help yourself—the more you help, the more the whole pie expands.

It also says that you have to act and believe in the whole process. If you think and act from a scarcity model, you will find scarcity. If the energy you put into the universe comes from the mindset that you can easily get what you need and more, that's what you're likely to find.

Saul Wilner, of 1-800-GRANOLA.com, has a "motivational equation" he calls CPR:

context = purpose + intended result.

If you know what you specifically want to achieve, and you know the broader reason for why you are in this venture, you can create the context to make those things happen. In his case, his purpose is to make a significant reduction in world hunger, his intended result is to double US consumption of granola by branding his phone number and website as the sales and fulfillment solution for many different granola companies, and the context he created to make this happen is something he calls the "Top It Off With Granola World Tour."

While it's too early in the process to report results, his program looks very promising.

The Abundance Model in Business

Lots of things change once you start looking at business through the "abundance filter." The biggest difference is that you don't need to feel threatened by your competitors. Because there is enough for all of you, you may even find that you want to cooperate. You can form alliances with others in your niche, and these alliances will be far more powerful than the group of you scrambling like mice to beat one other to the cheese—and never realizing that the cheese is inside a mousetrap.

Businesses that you partner with will be more eager to put their relationship with you ahead of less ethical companies. They know that a joint venture involving you will have fewer risks and more benefits; you are someone who can be trusted, and you won't be sucked into the abyss that swallowed Enron, WorldCom, or Arthur Andersen.

Most importantly, you benefit yourself. Your business thrives, you feel good about what you do, you build warm relationships based on the best human qualities. You walk the streets with a light heart and your head held high.

Listen for a moment to marketing copywriter and consultant B.L. Ochman:

> I used to be afraid to put news about my competitors' e-books, newsletters and teleconferences in my newsletter. But I've completely changed my mind. I have begun to promote my competitors' works and to include them in the affiliate program for my e-books. I do teleseminars with them.
>
> Why? There is plenty of work to go around. People looking for PR and marketing are going to shop around anyway so why deny that fact? We can refer work to each other and we can enjoy the halo effect of being associated with smart, accomplished people. Try it, you'll benefit.
>
> B.L. Ochman, BLOchman@whatsnextonline.com
> http://www.whatsnextonline.com

Huh—what just happened here? I just gave you the name and contact info of one of my competitors—I do all the same things that she does. And I've never met her and have never seen the work she does for her clients. Why on earth would I do that?

Maybe, just maybe, it's because I really believe in what I'm writing here. In fact, in the Resources section, you'll find a listing of "Clued-In Copywriters," all of whom are competitors of mine.

And B.L. believes it too; when I wrote for permission, she wrote back offering to review this book in her newsletter. Perhaps some of you saw it mentioned there.

And this philosophy really does pay back. A few months ago, B.L., who had been living just blocks from the World Trade Center in New York City, was having a fight with her ex-landlord; she'd had to move when her apartment became uninhabitable after 9/11, and the landlord was trying to retain many thousands of dollars that she would have paid in rent. She turned to her allies online, and within weeks, the pressure campaign she created accomplished the desired effect.

Now—I submit that the reason B.L. was able to get so much help from some of the world's heavy hitters in sales and marketing is because she had long ago established herself as a person who doesn't just take, but gives—again, operating out of that abundance mentality. If B.L. had been a cutthroat, if she had tried to steal business from her competitors or turn in useless work to her clients, would there have been a mass movement to come to her rescue? I strongly doubt it. First of all, she wouldn't have been known to the Internet communities where she turned for help. And second, people who had been burned would have sabotaged the campaign before it ever got out of the gate.

Let's look at another entrepreneur who has succeeded by embracing the abundance paradigm: Scottie Claiborne of Hullaballoo Entertainment. Recognizing that she was getting national and international traffic to her website <http://www.hullaballoorental.com> for a local service (rentals of kids' inflatable play equipment), she turned her site into a directory, where, no matter where you are, you can find the nearest vendor—and then she sought out other companies and asked them to list on her site. In other words, she drives traffic to businesses that could be thought of as her competitors. She believes that her listing of other sites is directly responsible for her Number 1 rank at Google, which in turn generates lots and lots of traffic directly.

The site was successful very quickly, and now she's branching out into selling the equipment to the other companies—all of whom know her company because she's been funneling inquiries to them![25]

---

25. Scottie Claiborne, "Links Are Good for Business," *High Rankings Advisor*, Nov. 20, 2002 <http://www.highrankings.com/advisor.htm>.

7

Examples of Success

Many successful companies use everyone-wins strategies. Here are a few among hundreds I could cite. If they can do it, so can you.

Saturn

It wasn't so many years ago that buying a car was a horrible chore. You came into the dealership fully expecting a hostile, manipulative environment. But even before the Internet made it possible for consumers to be far better informed, Saturn revolutionized the way cars are sold—and sold a huge number of cars in the process.

Saturn is a part of General Motors, the largest US car maker, and one firmly rooted in the old, adversarial ways. But Saturn did a number of things differently. It created a feeling of pride and ownership among its employees that enabled the car line to quickly develop a reputation for quality. Its design standards emphasized safety but did not compromise value, economy, performance, or comfort. And the Saturn dealer network—many of whom also operated traditional showrooms selling other brands—treated the customer as a valued part of not just the sales process but the entire idea of driving a Saturn. The "customer really counts" philosophy even extends to its ads, which have often featured ordinary people who drive Saturns.

When you walk into a Saturn dealer, you get a friendly greeting and you're told who can answer your questions. There's no pressure. Your contact will helpfully assess your needs and suggest a vehicle that will work for you. And if you decide to buy, the price is already set—at a level that provides very good value to the consumer and very good profit to the dealer.

It's all spelled out in the "Saturn Consultative Sales Process," which says, among other things, "All customers shall receive a thorough interview in order for Sales Consultants to determine their wants and needs" and "All customers shall receive open and honest treatment about all elements of the transaction price."

Since Saturn introduced its new dealership style in the early 1990s, many other dealerships have followed suit. But from them, it seems like imitating a successful marketing technique; in Saturn, it's part of the culture, and of the success.[26]

In JD Power & Associates' annual automotive sales satisfaction study, Saturn has ranked Number 1 seven out of the last eight years. It's the only nonluxury brand to earn top ranking in both Power's Customer Service and Sales Satisfaction indexes; the only other brand that achieved both the same year was Lexus, in 1994.[27]

The company continues to grow. November 2002 sales were up 16.9 percent over November 2001, even as overall GM vehicle sales declined 18 percent over the previous November.[28] Jill Lajdziak, Saturn vice president of sales, service, and marketing, expected cumulative 2002 sales to be 10 percent above 2001's, and by 2005 she expects to nearly double the number of units sold.[29]

Nordstrom

How did Nordstrom become one of the largest department stores, opening numerous new locations while some of the world's greatest store names went out of business? It certainly wasn't on low prices!

Nordstrom built a reputation for excellent service—for going so far out of their way to assist customers that the company's reputation for excellence spread far and wide.

Living in an area where Nordstrom hadn't reached yet, I first learned about the company from Guy Kawasaki's book, *The Macintosh Way*, in the

26. In fairness to the old paradigm, auto industry analyst Jim Ziegler told me in a telephone interview, on Dec. 11, 2002, that although the no-negotiation rule makes the dealerships very profitable, GM has heavily subsidized the division, driving down the price of the cars and taking a loss of about a billion dollars per year. Read his highly opinionated views at: <http://www.zieglersupersystems.com/new%20web/dealermag/back_to_the_future.htm> and <http://www.zieglersupersystems.com/new%20web/dealermag/a_cornered_dog.htm>.
27. "Saturn Honors 11 Retailers for Exceptional Performance," Aug. 21, 2002 <http://www.saturnfans.com/Company/2002/2002summitaward.shtml>.
28. "November Sales Up 16.9%," Dec. 3, 2002 <http://www.saturnfans.com/Company/2002/november2002sales.shtml>.
29. "Saturn Eyes 500,000 in Sales by 2005," Dec. 3, 2002 <http://www.saturnfans.com/Company/2002/500000sales.shtml>.

1980s. He cited several examples of excellence, and Nordstrom was among them. The store has been known to accept returns of heavily used merchandise that probably wasn't even bought there; but instead of focusing on short-term profits, the company went after long-term consumer loyalty and word-of-mouth brand building. If you return an item of clothing that no sensible store would take back, and you get full credit, aren't you going to shop there over and over again—and tell your friends?

Stop & Shop Apple Promotion

A lot of years ago, Stop & Shop, a large New England supermarket chain, teamed up with Apple Computer for a very innovative promotion. Many others have copied it since (and for all I know, Stop & Shop may not have been the first)—because it created huge customer loyalty for both companies and also helped the communities where it was offered.

Customers turned their register receipts in to their children's schools. The schools counted the dollars spent toward points, redeemable for computer equipment from Apple. Of course, Stop & Shop drew customers from other stores—and Apple trained new users in its own operating system from a young and tender age. Since the Apple operating system has less than 10 percent of the market, this campaign established a vital new base of Apple-oriented computer buyers, who would be buying systems of their own in a few years.

Stop & Shop had another great win–win powerhouse a few years later: a no-fee frequent-flier credit card that earned a mile for every dollar spent, and two miles for every dollar spent at Stop & Shop. Unfortunately, after about four years, the sponsoring bank was bought out by a large conglomerate that eventually killed the program. But many of those former airline customers stayed with the grocery chain out of habit.

Other Affinity Promotions

Many other businesses have teamed up with schools, offering books, supplies, training, and other benefits at certain dollar levels. And many businesses and nonprofit organizations have also benefited from affinity programs of one sort or another. Working Assets was perhaps the first to team up a long-distance telephone plan with a social benefit to political organizations that its members support—in this case a pool of organizations selected by the members, each of which receives a substantial contribution. Now there are a number of others, including at least one company whose phone plan is actively sold by the members of the beneficiary organizations—and each person who signs up benefits the group under which he or she was signed up. For instance, the National Writers Union (of which I'm a member) offers a phone plan, and the NWU gets a percentage on all its members who participate. Members are encouraged to refer their nonmember friends, too.

And, of course, there are affinity credit cards—sometimes it seems every college alumni association must have one. All of these work because they provide ways for members to help the organization, just through the purchases they already make.

Johnson & Johnson: A Lesson in Ethical Crisis PR

In 1982, seven people died after consuming tampered-with, cyanide-laced packages of Extra-Strength Tylenol—a popular seller for Johnson & Johnson. The company's response was immediate—and consumer-focused. Although the poisonings were localized and specific to one product, the company took no chances. It recalled all Tylenol products, nationwide—31 million bottles, worth over $100 million—and offered a $100,000 reward.[30]

The company clearly put consumer safety ahead of its own profits. Though the loss was substantial, the resulting gain in consumer confidence allowed the company to recover quickly, and gain wide respect.

Clearly, the company actually follows its own credo, which orders its responsibities: consumers first, then employees, then local and world communities, and lastly, stockholders.[31]

Contrast this firm commitment to ethics with some of the slippery tactics of other companies recently facing a safety scare—such as Ford and Bridgestone/Firestone, which created PR and sales disasters for themselves by attempting to duck responsibility for SUV rollover accidents.[32]

30. As chronicled on Oh No News, a fascinating website of "Images and News that make company executives go OH NO!"<http://www.ohnonews.com/tylenol.html>.
31. The full credo can be found at <http://www.jnj.com/our_company/our_credo/index.htm>.
32. Ford officials discussed the problem even as far back as May 1, 1987, while the Explorer was still in the design phase. The story reached the US press in a report by CBS affiliate KHOU, of Houston—long after Ford had already recalled tires in Malaysia, Saudi Arabia, and elsewhere. Public Citizen, a watchdog group founded by Ralph Nader, offers a detailed chronology at <http://www.citizen.org/autosafety/firestone/articles.cfm?ID=5336> (downloaded January 16, 2003).

8

Joint Ventures, Big and Small

Some of the examples just described are actually joint ventures—a fancy phrase that simply means working together with another business. JVs might range from a simple comarketing deal like stuffing fliers for each other in outbound orders, all the way up to a full-scale corporate merger. In between, there are many steps on the ladder: project-specific partnerships, bundling products from different companies to add value, handing out a freebie from another business as an incentive award, and on and on it goes.

Since, for many people, the idea of working with a competitor is strange and peculiar, we'll start with some examples that show how very easy it actually is to work with people in the same field. Then we'll look at some more everyone-wins JVs for businesses that don't compete directly.

Turn Your Competitors into Allies

1. Get to know the other people in your niche. When you notice a new arrival in the marketplace—or if you enter a market new to you—pick up the phone and get acquainted. Become active in trade associations in your industry, and in your geographic area (for example, Chamber of Commerce, neighborhood business association). Participate in Internet discussion groups with others in your own or closely related fields. Talk shop, discuss approaches to problems, let each other know about events or opportunities of interest. Know each company's Unique Selling Proposition (USP)—the key reason why it makes sense to do business with that company—and that way, you'll know when and where to refer accounts that aren't quite right for you.

2. Market together, cooperatively. I remember a wonderful newspaper co-op

ad from all my local florists, who teamed up just before Mother's Day. The headline: "You wouldn't buy your groceries from a *florist!* So, why buy your plants from a *grocer?*" The ad copy emphasized higher plant quality, expert knowledge, and various other benefits, and then listed full contact info for 11 different flower shops.

By joining forces, the consortium could afford a big, noticeable ad. An ad one-eleventh the size would have been easy to ignore, but this one filled a quarter-page (in a large-format newspaper) and demanded to be noticed.

Another example: in publishing, many small presses will include a flier for a complementary book from another publisher as they ship out orders; for the very low cost of printing and mailing the fliers, participating publishers get to reach an entirely new audience. Sometimes, publishers will even sell a bundle consisting of their own and other firms' books, gathered together at a value price.

It's not just small companies doing this, either. Some of the largest and most fiercely competitive corporations in the world engage in joint ventures regularly. The first car I ever bought new was a 1988 Chevrolet Nova, which was essentially identical to the Toyota Corolla. Built by Chevrolet to Toyota's specification, it was a marvelous car, and about $2000 less than the same car with the Toyota nameplate. Fifteen years after production ended, I still see a lot of them on the road. Similarly, the popular Ford Escort wagon was really a Mazda, etc., etc.

Think about the package delivery business. FedEx and the United States Postal Service have a very interesting arrangement; the USPS subcontracts intercity air transportation of Express Mail and Priority Mail to FedEx, which gets a substantial new revenue stream and utilizes otherwise wasted air freight capacity. And meanwhile, FedEx has installed thousands of drop boxes at post offices around the country, thus helping its consumers avoid pick-up charges and making shipping with the company incredibly convenient.[33]

For service businesses, sometimes your biggest competitor is not another company, but the idea of doing it yourself. Certainly, this is true in my business. Most people believe they can write well—and few of them understand the difference between putting sentences together on paper to convey

33. William Pride and O. C. Ferrell, *Marketing Concepts and Strategies*, 12th ed. (Boston: Houghton Mifflin, 2003), p. 56.

information—something most people can actually do themselves—and writing materials with a sharply defined focus and a powerful call to action, or a news hook. Only a very small percentage of businesses ever hire outside professional copywriters. Large firms hire this skill internally, and many small firms use their own (untrained) marketing departments.

In my business, two of the largest revenue streams are marketing copywriting and résumé writing. On the résumé side, our "market share" went down sharply after large numbers of people started having access to PCs and laser printers, and it went down dramatically again after Microsoft started bundling a résumé template in Microsoft Word. During the boom times when companies would hire any warm body, people could get by with that approach. But now, in a leaner economy, many of our résumé clients bring a document they created in this template—because it hasn't been landing job interviews. We can easily see why these self-written résumés haven't been working; they don't properly highlight the client's strengths or minimize weaknesses, the format may not be appropriate, and the writers haven't focused their résumé on their target market: people who hire employees with a particular skill set.

3. Refer business to each other. Typically, you will each have areas of specialization that you do better than others. So if you get an inquiry from someone best served by your competitor, you satisfy the customer by playing matchmaker. And your competitors will do the same for you. I have some competitors—and complementary businesses—with whom I pay or charge a referral commission, and others where we simply pass appropriate clients to each other.

My business started primarily as a typing service, but very quickly, I branched out into writing résumés and marketing materials. I joined a local association of secretarial services, and because people knew my specialties, I got a lot of résumé work through referrals.

At the same time, after my first two tape-transcription assignments, I decided I really disliked that part of the business and began referring those jobs out to other services.

This cooperation always had three winners: the client, of course, who got the best providers for the services they needed; but also my competitors and me: we didn't let the things we disliked get in the way of doing what we enjoyed and excelled at, yet we were able to keep our clients happy when they requested those services.

Here's another one of my "competitors," Wendy Kurtz, MBA, APR, CPRC, president of the PR firm Elizabeth Charles & Associates <http://www. elizabethcharles.com>, talking about how this works for her:

> I disagree with the premise that there are only two types: winners and losers. All too often, we as professionals tend to overlook the basic concept we learned in childhood, "Do unto others as you would have them do unto you." I have found that some of my best referrals have come from vendors and those competitors with whom I maintain a sense of "we're in this together," rather than "we're out to beat each other to the top."[34]

4. Subcontract with each other. If one of you has too much work and the other has too little, doesn't it make sense to work with a professional that you trust and even it all out?

5. Create temporary joint ventures, where each of you is a partner. After all, if fierce competitors like Apple and IBM could join together (with Motorola as a third partner) to develop the Power PC chip architecture, surely you and your competitors can put aside your differences. These could be equal or weighted partnerships.

6. In some cases, if you work so well together, and enjoy advantages of scale, increased buying power, and so forth—and your corporate cultures harmonize well with each other—a permanent merger or acquisition may even make sense.

7. Be there if your competitors fold; if you've maintained strong positive relations, if you've cooperated on several projects, if your competitor leaves the business, *you* will get the referrals.

In the earliest days of my business, one of my competitors called me up and asked me if I needed any office supplies; he wanted to place an order with a large mail-order wholesaler and didn't have enough to make the minimum. That phone call has saved me thousands of dollars, because I wasn't aware of this very inexpensive supplier. I not only added my order to his, but for the past 20 years I've ordered from that company—at a deep discount over anything I could find locally.

---

34 *I-PR Digest*, Oct. 22, 2002 <http://www.adventive.com>.

And yes, this competitor later moved out of the area. He was one of several who sent all their clients to me when they closed their shops.

I got the initial call—*and* the later referrals—because we were on friendly terms and had often sent each other clients.

You've Done the Hardest Part—Now, Network with Complementary Businesses

Psychologically, it may be pretty hard, at first, to accept the idea that your competitors can be extremely powerful allies in growing your business. That's why I put competitors first in this section. I wanted you to see that these techniques work even with the people you might have thought you were least likely to develop partnerships with. The ideas in these next subsections will seem really easy after you've already started thinking about how you and your competitors can help each other.

If your business uses a retail model—you have a storefront or office where your customers and clients come to you—geographically based partnerships make a lot of sense. It is in everyone's interest to draw people into the area where your business is located. And that area can be as small as a single office building, a strip mall, a city block—or as big as an entire state or country. This is why Chambers of Commerce and neighborhood business associations get organized, why economic development offices and tourism departments promote their region as a place to locate or visit. But that's only the beginning.

Some other ways to cross promote:

- Organize and promote a special event that draws traffic. It could be as simple as a group promotion with 20 percent off any one item, or as complex as a street fair with live concerts, children's activities, dignitaries, and so forth.

- Market the neighborhood or region as a destination. In Minneapolis, the many restaurant owners along Nicollet Avenue banded together and dubbed it "Eat Street"; they even posted permanent banners proclaiming this to all who pass by—and even people who live in distant suburbs recognize the destination.

- Seek partnerships with complementary businesses in the neighborhood: *Cooperative Life Leader* magazine reports that a food co-op in Durham, New Hampshire, invited the weekly farmers' market to set up shop outside the store.[35] The existing storefront provided a natural base for the farm stands, and other people seeking fresh produce were drawn into the store to buy other natural foods.

Join with your neighbors to advertise the neighborhood. There are many ways to do this: list several businesses in one ad; give more space to one business at a time, rotating through all the members; create and distribute a group flier, website, ad-supported map, catalog, or discount coupon book...

Organize together under an association banner for neighborhood improvement projects—anything from a group litter-pick up to creating public pressure to close down health and safety hazards—and tell the media what you're doing.

If there's a major attraction nearby, work with the local tourism bureau to develop a brochure about other nearby attractions (including yours) that the large attraction can distribute; the participants can reciprocate, of course.

Geographical proximity is only one possible bridge to collaboration. If you're in a service business, especially, you may be able to partner with complementary services. For instance, wedding planners, caterers, banquet halls, photographers, florists, and musicians can cooperate to provide a one-stop wedding service. And if your business is not local, your partnerships can spread out as well; the person who maintains my websites is based in Alaska, thousands of miles away from me.

The partnership can be active or passive—and sometimes can lead to whole new opportunities. I had brought a marketing-savvy graphic artist in to collaborate on a number of client projects. She then brought me into a three-way arrangement with a local Web designer to produce some collateral and a website for our local Board of Realtors; we all went up to the group's offices to present ourselves. The organization had asked the Web designer to register a very obscure domain name that only had meaning for them. When we heard the domain name, the graphic artist and I exchanged looks, and we started telling the organization why the domain they'd picked would be a marketing disaster. I told the executive director to imagine giving out that name on the radio, and to look at a name that would reinforce the group's identity and message. This was a free consulta-

35. Electronic edition, Sept. 2002. Published by the Cooperative Development Institute, Greenfield, Mass. <http://www.cooplife.com/>.

tion; we didn't even know if we had the job yet. But we all brainstormed a bunch of better domain names—and then a few months later I got a call from the president of the largest real estate firm in the service area. He had been impressed at that meeting and came to me to rewrite the firm's entire collection of a dozen or so brochures—a very juicy assignment. By advising the client that its course was strewn with obstacles, I had put myself in the position to receive a much, much larger assignment, one for which I was not competing against any other copywriters.

That three-way collaboration is a happy example of active partnership—and the only one I can remember participating in where all the contractors met with the client, together. Most of my JV relationships have actually been far less formal. As a copywriter who writes press releases but doesn't send them out or follow them up, I have recommended vendors who provide these services—and, for that matter, graphic design, search engine optimization, website coding, etc. And not necessarily tit for tat, but looking at "what goes around comes around," I get quite a bit of work referred to me by other professionals who offer similar, but not the same, services. These have taken one of three models, and I'm not fussy about which model:

- Informal referrals, in which no money changes hands
- Formal referrals, where the receiving business owner pays a commission (typically, 10 percent on the first order)
- Subcontractor relationships, where just one business works directly with the client, and farms out other services as needed (in some cases marking up the subcontractor's service)

One More Step—Turn Your Customers and Suppliers into Evangelists

If mutual-success cooperative approaches work so well horizontally, with competitors, won't they also work vertically? The people who choose to do business with you, and the people with whom you choose to do business, are natural allies.

Here are a few ideas:

1. Use testimonials in your advertising, or submit testimonials to other businesses. If you're satisfied with a product or service, offer a testimonial for

that company's ads. Jim McCann's wildly successful 800-FLOWERS was plugged in national TV and print ads by AT&T—because McCann praised the telecommunications giant's toll-free service. It would have cost him millions of dollars to get the exposure if he'd paid for it himself.

On a much smaller scale, years ago, I offered a local telephone book publisher this plug:

> I track my sources of clients, and Yellow Pages advertising brings in about 70% of them. Right now, I'm in the Pioneer Valley book and three Nynex books. Amazingly enough, Pioneer Valley is outpulling all three Nynex books combined. Keep up the good work!
>
> Shel Horowitz, Author, *Marketing Without Megabucks: How to Sell Anything on a Shoestring*; Director, Accurate Writing & More, Northampton, MA

Not only did the company run this testimonial in local papers—and yes, I heard from several people who saw it—but it also showed its gratitude by throwing in a few hundred dollars in upgrades to my own ads in its book. Meanwhile, I got my name, my firm name, and my then-current book plastered all over the phone book's three-county circulation area.

Not a bad deal for something that took about three minutes to write and maybe thirty minutes to negotiate.

If you do print or broadcast advertising anyway, and if your clients say nice things about you, ask permission to use their quote in your ads—and if the ad is on radio or TV, ask if they'll let you tape them reading the quote. (For ideas on how to get really great testimonials, please see my book, *Grassroots Marketing: Getting Noticed in a Noisy World*).

I've long been a believer in the marketing power of testimonials, endorsements, and referrals. These tools allow your customers, others in your networks, and perhaps even celebrities, to do your marketing for you.

In the early days of my own business, we began actively asking our clients to pass our name around. Each person who came to my office left with a business card; as my wife or I handed out the card, we'd say, "If you have friends or colleagues who need this service, please spread the word." And sometimes, the client would turn to us and say, "I actually know several people. May I have a few more cards?"

We continue this strategy today, two decades later. This simple remark is part of why fully half of the clients who come to our office are either referred by existing clients or are coming back after a previous happy experience with us.

For those clients who work with me over the Internet rather than in person, the percentage is even higher. My largest source of new clients these days is a certain e-mail discussion list of small-press publishers. I've made it a practice to ask people who've used and been delighted by my services to mention their satisfaction to the list (some of them do so anyway, without any prompting from me). So over a period of years, participants in this list have heard dozens of people exclaim about my skills in writing promotional materials, even on tight deadlines. Some of these publishers may go months or years between new titles. But when they have a new book coming out, they need to find someone to write their publicity. I post frequently and helpfully to this group, and many of my posts subtly demonstrate (often by using examples from client work I've done) the advantages of having press releases professionally written—something that's particularly true in the book industry, where it's very hard to get press coverage through "ordinary" press releases. And at the end of my post is my signature, an electronic business card that mentions my writing services, along with contact information and the slogan, "I make the world *insist* on learning why *you're* special." (To keep it fresh, I do change the signature every once in a while, or use one of the many alternate versions I've developed.)

Here's an actual example (trimmed a bit): an e-mail I wrote to the list on May 16, 2002:

> Just opened an envelope from [a list member and client] to discover a review of his book. Other than two paragraphs added at the beginning, it's almost identical to the press release I wrote...
>
> This is not all that unusual. In fact, the one time I saw a *New York Times* story covering a book I'd written about, I was amused to see that this bylined article by a well-known columnist (no, I won't mention names!) took several entire paragraphs straight out of my release...

That's OK! That means that *I* did my job right and the journalist thought it was good enough. I am long past the need to see my own byline attached to my words...

So what's the lesson here?

Lesson 1: When sending out book press releases, always send your best work. Not only does it increase the chances of coverage, but it may be used essentially as is. Lesson 2: Never send anything you'd be ashamed of if it landed in print.

The unspoken Lesson 3 is, "Shel's press releases are so good that a reporter for the *New York Times*—probably the toughest paper in the nation to get media coverage in—lifted large portions and plopped it into an article. Shel can write you a press release that could get noticed and used by major media." But I didn't have to beat my readers over the head with that information; it was there as part of a long-term relationship of trust and expectation of quality that I have built as an active member of this list.

A publisher in the final stages of bringing out a new book sees this message and signature, remembers all the previous posts from others about my excellent skills, quick service, and affordable prices—and I get a call or an e-mail asking if I can do some writing.

Believe it or not, this list brings me thousands of dollars a year with no monetary investment at all. Often it will start with a very small job, perhaps a single press release—but as clients realize that my approach really helps them market more successfully, they come back for many other projects. Some of the people on this list have done many thousands of dollars worth of business with me, and again, my marketing cost for these clients was zero.

One of my clients was somewhat skeptical about whether my approach was actually better than what he'd been doing on his own. So he ran a test. He sent out a press release I'd written to one group of journalists, and one of his own press releases to another set. He reported back to the entire list that my release had pulled six times as many responses as his own effort. He has since come back to me for many, many projects, and I'm sure the glowing reports he gave helped other clients decide to contact me.

This is not just my own experience, either. Many vendors who participate in this list—designers, editors, and at least one intellectual property lawyer, among others—find that list-mates account for a substantial percentage of their client load. Nor is it something found only on this particular list. At least as far back as 1995, writers like Marcia Yudkin and Jay Levinson were writing about this technique in their books on online marketing.[36] In fact, I talked about this method, in general terms, in a book I wrote back in 1991.[37]

And marketing via e-mail lists gets even better: I have actually gotten a number of referrals from members of this list who have *not* used my services themselves. But after years of seeing my helpful posts and my clients' glowing praises of my work, they are delighted to give my name out.

This is a form of viral marketing, to use the phrase popularized by Seth Godin in his book *The Idea Virus*. Viral marketing uses resources far beyond the marketer's own organization to spread the message very rapidly, much as a virus spreads through close physical contact. The classic case is Hotmail, which, by advertising its free e-mail services at the bottom of every outbound message from one of its users, grew amazingly rapidly.

Hotmail is the fastest growing subscription-based service in world history, achieving an astonishing 12 million subscribers in its first year and a half. About 150,000 new users sign up every day—and give the company significant demographic information about themselves. Hotmail is now the largest e-mail provider in the world, dwarfing even America Online. Microsoft bought it a while back.

Its nearest competitor in the free e-mail arena, a service called Juno, has only about a third as many users. Yet Hotmail spent only $500,000 on marketing to achieve its first 12 million members; Juno, in contrast, spent $20 million.[38]

The difference? Hotmail pioneered the tagline ad and got the first-mover advantage.

My second-largest source of marketing clients is a PR shop whose services complement mine. We pay each other commissions for client referrals,

36. Marcia Yudkin, *Marketing Online* (New York: Plume/Penguin, 1995); Jay Conrad Levinson and Charles Rubin, *Guerrilla Marketing Online* (Boston: Houghton Mifflin, 1995).

37 Shel Horowitz, *Marketing Without Megabucks: How to Sell Anything on a Shoestring* (New York: Simon & Schuster, 1993), pp. 195-196. I turned in the manuscript in December 1991, and it was published in May 1993. I still have a few left, but all the information there is also in my newer and more comprehensive book, *Grassroots Marketing: Getting Noticed in a Noisy World*.

38. "Viral Marketing" by Steve Jurvetson and Tim Draper, *Business 2.0*, Nov. 1998 <http://www.dfj.com/files/viralmarketing.html>.

and over the last year or so, we've passed the same dollars back and forth a number of times.

Much-published marketing author Marcia Yudkin, citing a booklet by sales consultant Paul Johnson called "Let Your Customer Sell You," talks about the art of asking for small favors: once someone gives you a testimonial, he or she has made an emotional commitment to you and your product. And the person who has done you a small favor may then be more willing to do you a larger favor.[39]

If the favor is a testimonial, your clients not only publicly state their commitment, but also cement the reasons why they felt so good about you in their own minds. You may well get more referrals, or more work assignments.

Johnson believes that one of the best times to get a testimonial is when you haven't heard from the client in a while, so he or she remembers the value you created. But I disagree; I think it's better to get the testimonial while the fabulous job you did is still on the front edge of the client's consciousness. Were I looking to attract more business from the source of the testimonial after a long absence, I'd take a different approach. For instance, send a quick note—perhaps accompanied by a small gift or a discount coupon for a future order—that says, "I just wanted to thank you again for your beautiful testimonial, reprinted below. For six months, it has helped me turn prospects into clients. I'm honored and gratified by your continued faith in my work."

David Frey, one of America's unsung marketing geniuses and author of *Marketing Best Practices* (see Resources section), reminded me that you can use your clients and customers as case studies, and write articles or white papers about them. If you publish articles in magazines, you're not paying for advertising; with many publications, you even get paid. Again, they get exposure, you get exposure, and you show how you've solved a problem for them. (Get their written permission ahead of time, of course.)

Frey also suggests giving out an award to a big customer or supplier; by so doing, you can build brand awareness, customer retention, and the opportunity for quite a bit of publicity and marketing oomph.

2. Explore co-op advertising programs, where a supplier partially subsidizes the cost of a retailer's ads and in-store displays. Many manufacturers will

39. Reported in Yudkin's e-mail newsletter, "The Marketing Minute," Sept. 25, 2002.

provide logos, sales aids, and actual dollars to help you tell the world that you carry their products. You can sometimes also get this kind of help from credit card companies, retail co-ops, professional associations, and so on.

3. Institute loyalty, referral, and incentive programs that keep your customers coming back. These programs can be very simple—for instance, a business card that gets punched for every purchase, and after ten punches, the customer gets a gift (often, a free copy of the product). Or they can be quite complex, involving several suppliers, multiple locations, and complex rewards.

These programs offer wonderful opportunities to partner with other merchants. Find complementary businesses whose offerings will resonate with your customers; you offer a reward from the other store, which in turn rewards its own customers with something from you. This is something even some of the country's largest corporations do. For instance, a cereal box may have a coupon good for a bottle of juice from a different company, or a fill-up at a gas station gets you a deep discount on a car wash. Use goods and services from other businesses as rewards in your loyalty and incentive programs, and then you have the benefit of reaching their customers as well as your own.

You can operate similar programs, not only to reward your own customers for frequency and amount of purchase, but also to actively solicit referrals. If a customer sends you a customer, it's nice to say thank you! In my business, usually the thank-you is all I do. But if someone sends a whole bunch of clients, I may make a small gift. And unlike the frequency reward, where it makes the most sense to bring in other businesses, here's a perfect time to use your own offerings as a reward, so that your own client comes back to you again. In my own business, I may give one of my books as a thank-you to a marketing client who has sent me a large amount of business—or, on the career side, free lifetime storage of the referring client's résumé. This costs me nothing out of pocket, but it could save the client a considerable amount of money over several years, *if* that same client comes back for an update.

If one of your sales staff has been a super-achiever, a reward is certainly appropriate (set it up as a policy, with performance levels quantified, so you can't get accused of favoritism). To create incentives within your own organization, partnering with other businesses once again expands the market for everyone. If you're friendly with a restaurant owner, see if he or she will donate a free dinner for two as a sales achievement award in exchange for publicity in your company newsletter and on your website. (As a side note, you can use this strategy in your outbound marketing, too. Donate a door prize to your local Chamber networking event, for example.)

4. Bundle complementary products and/or services together. Make life easier on your customers by arranging to provide all the pieces of the right solution, even when that means pulling them together from different vendors. Enhance your offer by combining complementary products that add value, for less money than buying them all separately. And of course, all the participating suppliers share the marketing cost, and all benefit by reaching each other's customers.

Here's a real-life example. To compete with integrated software that includes all these functions, four different software companies bundled together a word processor, spreadsheet, database, and graphics package. The word-processing company coordinated marketing. The same company also sold the word processor separately but added a free grammar checker.

Using the same principles, a carpenter, plumber, electrician, and painter could offer a one-stop home repair clearinghouse; rental car, airline, and hotel chains could join forces to offer a great one-stop deal for business travelers; a used-car dealer could team up with a car wash and an oil changer—in short, the possibilities are limitless.

5. Network with organizations that service your customers, and become a preferred or endorsed supplier. When you provide products or services through an association, several wonderful things happen:

- You reach the organization's membership at no cost, through its newsletters, website, and other promotional materials—and sometimes, this could be tens of thousands of members

- You receive the organization's implied endorsement, and thus, the members are predisposed to choose you (and even recommend you to their own networks)

- The members benefit from a better price, while the organization can receive a donation or a sales commission—and because you had no marketing cost, this is an easy benefit to offer

6. Enlist your customers' help for programs that benefit both of you: environmental or charity initiatives, fundraising for independent stores, etc.

   As I'm writing this, a local bank has just announced that it will divide $50,000 among a number of local charities—and the bank's customers get to vote on how the money will be divided, by nominating their favorite charities. The bank will apportion the grants according to the number of votes, above a very low minimum number. But only customers can vote! Of course, if you don't already happen to have an account there, the bank will be glad to set one up—and needless to say, this bank will gain a lot of new accounts as people sign up to support their favorite charities.

   Earlier, we talked about other campaigns where businesses assist schools, human service agencies, and other worthy causes. People are always predisposed to become your customer if doing so helps the community in some tangible way. And if your offer is good enough that it could stand without the charity tie-in, you should be able to market it very successfully by stressing the community benefit. (Of course, if your prospects don't see your offer as a benefit to themselves as well, you'll have a much harder time making the campaign work. But if you can get your prospects to buy in to both the community benefit and their own self-interest, you should have a very easy time with the campaign.)

   This attitude can even help for-profit businesses without a charity tie-in, under the right circumstances. I know of many, many local, independently owned businesses that have turned to their customers for help staying afloat against predatory competitors or surviving other adverse circumstances (such as a fire). One common strategy is to turn to your customers to raise capital, by providing scrip (money that can only be used in your own business) worth more than the cost of buying it—so, for instance, you can sell $20 scrip that can be redeemed as $25 store credit. Of course, this only works for businesses that have a community spirit and are known not only to treat their customers as allies, but to create a truly special environment—business owners, in other words, who have been practicing the principles of this book from the moment they first opened.

9

How the Abundance Paradigm Eliminates the Need to Dominate a Market and Allows You to Better Serve Your Customers

Once you get rid of "I win = you lose," many new horizons open up. Cooperation can take the form of trade associations, referrals, virtual partnerships, subcontracting arrangements, and more. These are all different ways of structuring the same result: that with enough work to go around, you can help each other.

Professional associations offer a number of benefits: sharing resources through joint purchasing power, learning from those who've gone before—from both their successes and their failures or mistakes—building the overall market, or simply having someone you can comfortably talk shop with or ask for advice on a problem client.

And if you have too much work, consider hiring your competitors to subcontract; not only do you keep the client but you get the work done by someone you trust to do it right.

I've used a number of subcontractors, and also subcontracted my own services to other PR shops, who make a very nice commission for brokering the work.

Does it bother me that these shops are making money for the work that I do? Not at all. They are paying my standard price; what does it matter to me if they mark up my services? Alternatively, some shops turn the client over to me, but ask for a referral fee, which I pay as a percentage of the first project. Still others simply connect me with the client and figure that I will give referrals back—and it will all come out in the wash.

We've already talked about referrals, but why not take it to the next level: virtual partnerships? Here, you actually join forces with a competitor to do a project together, kind of like a joint venture except that you dissolve the partnership once the job is complete.

Say you're offered a project with a short deadline, too large for you to do completely within your own company. If you can work with other shops to do pieces of it, and then assemble the entire project together as a finished whole, everyone benefits. But if you can't cooperate, you'll either be forced to turn down the project or work under such pressure that you do a bad job and kill any future business with that account. Whether it takes the form of many people doing different parts of one task—for instance, translating a large book to get ready for an international conference—or complementary tasks—such as the plumbing, electrical, and cement work on a construction site—working together enables you to complete the job faster, spreads work around, and makes impossible deadlines not only possible but much less stressful (and more lucrative, since you can charge a premium for rush work).

The Death of "Market Share"

You hear it constantly: "We need to gain market share."

My question: "Why?"

I believe very strongly that if my business has enough, it's not a problem if others have enough as well, In fact, a rising tide is more likely to lift other boats; more for you may very well mean more for me as well.

Consider a famous case: PC operating systems. In the beginning, believe it or not, Apple pretty much owned the market. The Apple II line had dominance in both hardware and software, in large part because the first PC spreadsheet—VisiCalc—was available first on that platform. The rest of the PC market was divided among companies like Tandy, Commodore, and Kaypro. When IBM entered the hardware market in 1981, using chips made by Intel and bringing in a little-known company called Microsoft to supply the operating system, the equation changed, because IBM actively courted business software developers in a way that Apple and the others had not. All of a sudden, the personal computer world was flooded with much more powerful word processors, databases, accounting programs, and so on. Thus, the business community migrated to IBM's platform. When Apple came back into the fray in 1984, with the original Mac, it quickly made inroads in graphic design, publishing, and educational markets—but because there weren't any good databases, those businesses already on the

IBM platform tended to stay there, and businesses getting their first computer naturally chose IBM.

The computer war might still have gone either way. But then IBM did something very clever: the company opened its architecture. All of a sudden, many companies were making "IBM-compatible" computers, selling them cheaply, and driving a vast expansion of the overall market. IBM's market share went down—but its sales went up, because a smaller piece of a much larger number turned out to be larger than the largest piece of a smaller number. The small fry with shallow pockets went to clones. But those who valued IBM's reputation for quality and support, or who didn't want to be bothered when it turned out that some of the clones weren't actually all that compatible, were willing to pay IBM's premium price.

The Mac market stayed strong in certain areas, where factors such as the much faster learning curve, better graphics capabilities, or the ability to see work on the screen as it would appear in print were more important than the ability to crunch data (education, publishing, advertising, music, and video, for instance). But more and more offices bought computers, and they were mostly buying Intel.

It became essentially impossible to run a business without a computer. Then newer software required more powerful computers. Next, Windows (from the user's point of view, essentially a copy of the much friendlier Mac operating system) reached maturity right around the time the Internet became popular—and users demanded full color, fast processors, and large hard drives. And people bought again. And again.

Thus, by creating an entire new class of competitors, IBM helped itself. And Microsoft, supplying DOS and Windows operating system software[40] to IBM and all the clones, and productivity software to users on both the Mac and Intel platforms, was sitting pretty.

At one point, Microsoft had nearly 90 percent of the operating system market, leaving most of the remainder to Apple.[41] More recently, inroads

40. Yes, I know that technically, Windows is not an operating system—but it functions as if it is one.
41. Some analysts say Microsoft still has 90 percent of the market: One example: "The Desktop OS: Are There Real Alternatives to Microsoft?" *Information Week*, July 2, 2002 <http://www.informationweek.com/reports/IWK20020808S0001/>. However, this seems to be based on obsolete data, given the growth of various flavors of Linux (including those supplied by major players like IBM) and huge sales in recent years of newer Macintoshes. As far back as February 2001, computer publisher and analyst Tim O'Reilly estimated that Linux had pulled even with Macintosh <http://www.oreilly.com/ask_tim/msvlinux_0201.html>.

by Linux and other open-architecture systems have brought Microsoft's percentage down, but it's still the dominant player, by far. (Interestingly, even without selling operating systems, Microsoft has historically sold—and still sells—more software for the Mac than any other software maker.)[42]

Yet Apple Computer, with just 4.5 percent of the US market, made a $40 million profit on revenues of $1.5 billion in one recent quarter, and shipped 813,000 units.[43] In a year, that means profits of $160 million, revenues of $6 billion, and over 3 million computers sold.

Could you make a comfortable living on those numbers? With an installed base of tens of millions of users, the Apple OS should be a big, promising, and potentially lucrative market for software developers, too (except that Apple's policies toward developers seem almost predesigned to sabotage the company's chances). In fact, Apple—even when its installed base was only a few million—often served as a testing ground for some of the most popular business software out there: PageMaker, Quark XPress, Adobe Illustrator and Photoshop, and even Microsoft Excel were first piloted on the Mac platform and then rolled out to the admittedly much larger DOS/Windows world. Even AOL, which was originally developed for the Commodore 64, was ported to the Mac as a product called AppleLink long before it was available for Windows computers.

For a small developer that doesn't want to become another Microsoft, Apple's market—setting aside the difficulties Apple sets up in working with developers—would make a lot of sense. Just 1 percent of the market exceeds 30,000 units per year. For a $50 product sold at a 50 percent wholesale discount, that's net revenues of $750,000 per year. If 5 percent of Apple's customers buy your product, you have an almost $4 million business—nothing to sneeze at. And of course, on direct-to-consumer sales, you don't have to give 50 percent to the wholesaler.

Unfortunately for Apple—and I speak as a Mac user since 1984—the lack of good visual programming development tools, the lack of support from the company, and various other factors mean it's not enough to

---

42. See, for instance, "Bill Gates' Secret? Better Products," by Stan Liebowitz in the *Wall Street Journal*, Oct. 20, 1998: "In 1989, Microsoft Excel had a 90 percent share of the Macintosh spreadsheet market, but only a 10 percent share of the PC market. That same year Microsoft Word had a 51 percent share of the Macintosh word-processing market, but only 15 percent of the PC market" <http://www.independent.org/tii/news/liebowitz_wsj1.html>.

43. First quarter 2001, as reported by C|Net Tech News <http://news.com.com/2100-1040-885301.html>—the most recent figures I found in a Google search Sept. 2, 2002.

simply look at the market numbers. Development costs and headaches are far higher on the Mac side, and of course, the number of prospects is smaller. What Apple is running up against is the 80/20 rule. If a company can achieve 80 percent of its potential customers with 20 percent of the work, why should it spend 80 percent of its resources for the remaining 20 percent gain? That, and not market share, is the reason why few developers bring out innovative Mac-only products anymore.[44]

In a service business, market share is even less relevant than it is in manufacturing. In a product-based environment involving manufacturing or high-volume retail, there are economies of scale that allow a market leader to command more favorable terms than smaller competitors. But these simply don't apply in most service businesses. Every service business offers a USP. For a copywriting shop like mine, it might be the ability to deliver fast, effective copy with a quick turnaround. For a baker, it might be the luscious chocolate filling that only this one shop offers. For a lawn-care business, it's simply the time and trouble the homeowner saves by farming the work out to someone who will show up every two weeks and never need a reminder. And if a community has 50,000 lawns, and 200 lawn-care businesses each service 25 households a week, that still only serves one-fifth of the potential base. Even though the market may appear saturated, there's plenty of room to grow. Too, those 25 companies can spread to other product lines. Chances are, homeowners would be delighted to hire the lawn-care person they already know and trust to prune trees, remove leaves, set up a composting system, perhaps even plow snow in the winter.

This idea works in the real world, even with much larger entities. Which was the only US airline to show a profit in the aftermath of the World Trade Center attack? Southwest Airlines. In their history of the company written some years earlier, Kevin and Jackie Freiberg quote CEO Herb Kelleher:

> Market share has nothing to do with profitability. Market share says we just want to be big; we don't care if we make money doing it....To get an additional 5 percent of the market, some companies increased their costs by 25 percent. That's really incongruous if profitability is your purpose.[45]

44. This conclusion is based on years of listening to complaints by software developers on various e-mail lists. Eric Anderson of FutureThru Group, and Alan Canton of Pub 1-2-3 are two among many who have said it's too much bother to develop for the Mac.
45. Kevin and Jackie Freiberg, *Nuts! Southwest Airlines' Crazy Recipe for Business and Personal Success* (New York: Broadway Books, 1998).

Does this mean market share is *never* a consideration? Or that you can't attempt to grow your market share without being predatory? No, in both cases. When you enter a new market, you need to calculate whether it will be worthwhile for you—and that means figuring out how much you'll sell. If you're entering a market that already exists, you need to calculate what percentage of the market will shift to you, how you'll attract them, how you'll draw in new customers who hadn't yet seen a need for what you offer—in short, you'll need to have some idea of how large a piece of the market will become your customers. However, ultimately, the number you really need to look at is how much money you will make, and not how that number relates to your competitors' performance.

My friend Eric Anderson, president of the consulting and computer services firm FutureThru Group, Inc. <http://www.futurethru.com>, will disagree with me here; he believes market share is actually quite important—but note that we're actually not so far apart. He points out that market share has little to do with your competitors, and everything to do with your customers. And Eric happens to be the smartest analyst I know; I have tremendous respect for him even when he and I don't agree. Just to let you make up your own mind, here are some of his thoughts:

> Market share matters intensely. It may matter less in some areas, but in general, it is often a significant indicator of the financial leverage a product might have.
>
> For the last 20 years or so, I have been involved in the launch of maybe 100 new products at four different companies, from very small to quite large. In nearly every case, market share has merited at least some consideration, and in many cases, it was the prime consideration.
>
> At the FutureThru Group, we build websites and software to help clients manage their business. Invariably, one of the biggest questions in any development project revolves around the client's market share, and how the client forecasts its business growth.
>
> Too many people think market share is about their competitors. This is usually a mistake.

Market share is not about competition. Market share is about your customers, and it helps you in three ways.

First, market share trends tell a company how well it is continuing to serve its customers. Declining market share indicates there is a problem. It could be that service, quality, price or some combination has slipped. Declining market share is a warning to the company that it is doing something wrong someplace.

While increasing market share may indicate that a company is fulfilling customer needs, it is possible to "buy" short-term market share gains that hide underlying problems.

The second property that market share brings is the ability to innovate and to spread development costs across a greater base. For example, Company A has 60 percent of the market and Company B has 40 percent.

Both companies discover that 10 percent of the market want Enhancement X.

Because Company A has greater market share, it can spread the cost of the enhancement across a greater customer base than Company B. Company A then has a lower cost of producing the enhancement per unit sold than Company B. Company A can pass the savings along to customers and/or retain it as profit.

Finally, if external financing is a consideration, banks, other lenders, or outside investors are going to be concerned about market share. Investors want to make money on their investment, and market share provides an indication of the security of their investment. If you have a small market share or declining market share, the chances of raising outside funding, if it is needed, become increasingly difficult.

Eric's comments (Oct. 13, 2002) lead directly to the next chapter: some of the "hard cases" in the concept that market share is not a key determinant.

10

Exceptions: Are There Cases When Market Share Really Does Matter?

While, in many cases, the concept of market share actually gets in the way of success, there are situations where there really are winners and los-ers—we'll look at some examples in a moment. But even here, you can win the race through ethical behavior that leaves your opponent standing and your conscience intact. It's all too easy to fall back into the old ways—but once you go for throat-cutting, you poison your own well. Be the best, get the prize—and look at yourself proudly in the mirror afterwards.

Here are four situations where you have to at least modify the mutual success approach—but even so, it does still work.

Major Media

Media coverage would seem to be a zero-sum game. Although anyone can get into local newspapers or on small radio shows, the most coveted slots are quite a bit tougher. A newspaper or broadcast station has a finite amount of space; if you get in, someone else doesn't.

Still, over time, that finite space is actually quite expansive. If a TV show uses two guests per show, five shows per week, that's over 500 guests a year. Each newspaper feature writer might profile four people in a week; that's more than 200 a year—and the paper might employ a dozen feature writers, so you have 2400 chances each year in that paper.

As someone who averages over 50 media interviews a year and has been mentioned or featured in plenty of major media, I can tell you that you can get major media with a cooperative approach.

In fact, it's just about the only way I get media: by formulating my media contact materials to make it obvious that the media outlet's readers, listeners, or viewers will learn something interesting and/or be entertained. In some cases, it may even make sense to suggest other businesses that would also be good sources for a "roundup" story, or to assemble a panel for a TV or radio show or speaking event. You may even find that not only do you do your competitors a favor and get them free publicity, but that you're able to differentiate your USP even more clearly—you demonstrate the ways you are different from them.

What if a competitor gets the coverage? The old, ineffectual response would be to call up the editor and complain. And all that does is ensure that that journalist will *never* use you as a story source—unless it's bad news or a scandal.

Here's one among many more effective strategies: write a letter to the editor, thanking the publication for the good story about your subject area and volunteering some new angle. You get the exposure, you're noticed as someone with something to contribute, and you may well get the call the next time that topic is covered.

(In my book, *Grassroots Marketing: Getting Noticed in a Noisy World,* I go into extensive detail on how to gain media publicity—and how to turn that publicity to your advantage as you market your products and services.)

Extremely Limited or Saturated Markets

Another scenario that challenges the idea that everyone can win: when there aren't very many customers, and a sale to you means that someone else doesn't get one. If there are only ten customers in the world for what you do, you probably want all ten.

Have we finally come to a situation where marketing from the abundance paradigm doesn't work?

Even here, there are many ways to achieve your agenda and keep within your principles.

You can be like Microsoft or General Motors and buy out your competitors—that's certainly a win–win if you've made a fair offer.

A more affordable strategy is to make it clear that working with you has advantages to the client: better service, a more thorough understanding of the client's needs, a more favorable financing structure. Without putting your competitors down, you provide the information necessary for your prospects to choose you. The benefit extends to your customers, and you're not trashing your competitors, even if you're not actively working with them.

Here's an example from my own business. One of the services I offer is résumé writing. Ten years ago, it was the largest piece of my business. Now, it's down to a small fraction, and most of my energy goes elsewhere; we are competing not only with other shops but with do-it-yourselfers who now have most of the market. We get a lot of calls from people who are price shopping. As it happens, our prices in this market have been very, very good—but we want prospects to consider other factors, too. We say, "The other question you should be asking is, 'What are your qualifications?'"—and then we tell them ours. A lot of people book an appointment then and there after hearing our response to a question they hadn't even asked!

But still, situations will come up where a competitor is obviously better qualified than you to handle a particular client's circumstances. And that's where it's important to remember that you serve these clients best by referring them to another business. It doesn't take many referrals before those competitive business owners realize that while you will certainly attempt to close the sale when someone is considering you, you always have the client's interests at heart and that inspires you to refer the work to other shops when that's the best way to meet the client's needs.

Another strategy is to expand the market. At this point, résumés are a relatively small part of our business—but some years ago, it was most of our livelihood. Had the do-it-yourself phenomenon been as strong back then, I would have approached my local competitors and discussed a cooperative marketing campaign to show people why they should have it done instead of writing their own résumés. The ads and publicity materials, of course, would list all the contact info for the participating shops, and would expand the pie for all of us—just as this approach worked for the florists cited earlier.

The hospitality industry has clearly been successful with this approach, as these two examples demonstrate. Bed-and-breakfast reservation services are common; you travel to a city and either call the local reservation service or visit its website. When you contact the service, the reservationist knows which innkeepers have rooms available in what price ranges, can tell you which is the best fit for your needs, and will then take your reservation over the phone. On the restaurant side of the industry, many cities have organized massive cooperative promotions, such as a "taste" festival where dozens of restaurants offer small, inexpensive samples of their most popular dishes, and thousands of consumers go from booth to booth, trying new foods. After the festival is over, these people seek out the restaurants they liked and enjoy the full dining experience.

There are a number of other ways to cooperate with competitors for mutual benefit. Formal or informal associations can develop new markets for all members. As an example, say a group of writing instructors band together. Maybe the basic market for fiction and poetry workshops is fairly saturated, but the group hires an outreach person to open doors in corporate training, senior centers, prisons, and schools, to partner with college and university creative-writing programs, and to create a public relations campaign encouraging writing among sectors of the public that haven't tried it before. Thus the organization can create an elevator under all of its members' feet. Rather than carving up a small market into tiny slivers, the group expands the market collectively, and all its members benefit.

My chiropractor practices a particular approach to spinal care called Network Spinal Analysis. Network practitioners are a small subset of chiropractors in general; our area has dozens of chiropractors, but only about five who do Network. They do quite a bit of cooperative marketing, refer patients to each other, and choose each other to work on their own backs.

Another benefit-focused strategy is to diversify. Three times in the history of my business—first with term-paper typing, then with my wife's writing workshops, and finally with résumés—I found that a service line was very strong for a few years, but because of technology, saturation, or other factors, that market largely disappeared. In all three cases, by the time the market dried up, we had already been offering new products and services, and were not only able to recover but actually able to increase both our hourly rate and profitability in those new areas.

Would I go back to typing term papers, even if the market were still there? Definitely not! Every time there has been pressure on a market that I had previously relied on for the largest share of my income, I found a new, better, more enjoyable, more lucrative market—and had the opportunity to develop new skill sets that are much more in demand, and for which my clients cheerfully pay a good deal more money.

One final approach is to go after a niche. This is an excellent strategy when you're facing changing technology, or you're feeling pressed by a deep-pockets competitor.

Think back a hundred years. There were still many companies making horse-carriages and buggy whips, but cars were beginning to displace horse-carriages as the preferred mode of transportation. Still, even now, there is a place for a buggy whip or carriage manufacturer—to serve the tourist carriages that roam through New York's Central Park or New Orleans's French Quarter. It's a much smaller market, one that a mass manufacturer can't profitably serve. But for one or two companies that go after that market, it can be a nice, profitable niche.

I have a friend who is a hand-bookbinder. Although the vast majority of books are bound by high-speed machines, my friend never lacks for work: he restores old books for libraries and private collectors, and creates works of art out of new books. Once again, the industry couldn't support thousands of hand-bookbinders, but it does support dozens.

Predators

"So," I can hear you thinking, "Marketing That Puts People First is all well and good if you have competitors that think the same way. But what if your competitor is a cut-throat trying to drive you out of business? You can nicey-nice yourself right into bankruptcy!"[46]

If a Wal-Mart or Home Depot, with its vast purchasing power and predatory practices, moves into your territory, striving for total market share, how do you deal with that?

Interestingly enough, independent hardware stores and lumberyards continue to exist, despite pressure from homeowner superstores. Some of their survival has come from developing cooperative approaches. To name one example, they've formed purchasing co-ops that can purchase goods at competitive prices. If a single hardware store were to buy inventory on

---

46. This section owes much to the creative thinking of Patrick and Jennifer Bishop's *Money Tree Marketing*, a book that I recommend highly for its ideas on how to create mutual benefit scenarios in which you get paid to advertise your business by forming co-ops and resale deals of various sorts. Not all their strategies are in the mutual success/mutual assistance mode—in fact, there are quite a number with which I strongly disagree—but enough are that I'm happy to recommend it. See the Resources section for more on this book.

its own, it might actually be cheaper for the store's purchasing manager to go to Lowe's or Home Depot and buy at retail. But by joining co-ops like Service Star or Tru-Value, they not only gain enough marketing muscle to buy cheaply, but also get the benefits of a national or regional brand.

When competing with a Wal-Mart—or, for that matter, a BJ's or Costco—the local stores that thrive are those that don't get into a price-cutting game. Lacking the ability to purchase warehouse quantities, they look to compete on value, not price; they find the places they can offer better service to their customers than the giants can, stress the importance of community-based retailing, and show the win-win advantages of a strong local-business sector.

Of course, if you've created a brand new market, your calculations need to be figured differently: how many people will you convince of the desirability of your new approach, and how long will you have before other companies move into the territory you've created?

We've already discussed some ways to survive and thrive when a large, well-financed competitor enters the market. But sometimes, with someone who is actively trying to own the entire market, you need a tougher approach. If a competitor comes in determined to drive you out, and brings a huge amount of firepower to bear, you certainly need a response. And in all likelihood, you won't have the budget to fight fire with fire. When you face massive ad campaigns in the Yellow Pages, local newspapers, and electronic media, you're not going to be able to spend your way out, because the other business may have deeper pockets—or a willingness to lose money until it can drive competitors out and "own" the market.

So what's a small-business owner to do? How can you survive an onslaught by a well-funded competitor who doesn't understand that there's enough to go around?

HERE ARE TWO EXCELLENT APPROACHES:

1. Identify and *use* the communication strategies where you're better than they are.

   You have your customer list; now's a great time to do some postal or electronic direct mail. *You* have carefully built up local contacts in the press. Explain to these contacts how you'll meet this new challenge—and what it would mean to the community if you can't. *You* have the benefit of your existing store traffic while the new competitor is under construction; think about how you can create allies out of those visitors. *You* have access to nimble, innovative marketing methods that a nonlocal superstore chain simply cannot use, because they have to spend months learning about them and then seeking approval from headquarters. *You* can compete as an equal, perhaps a superior, in cyberspace—because *you* can spend the time to optimize your pages for your own local area, for your own special product mix and USP, and for the value that you add to the equation when a customer chooses to do business with you.

2. Try a little marketing jujitsu! In jujitsu, you use your opponent's greater strength and redirect it so that your opponent, and not you, feels the brunt of the blow. In jujitsu, you can flip someone much larger than you over your shoulder and onto the mat. So, in a situation where your competitor insists that there is a winner and a loser, you want to be the winner.

Here's where the "political capital" you've built up over time can really help. If you have been in business several years, filling a unique niche in a special way that's meaningful to your community...if you've been regularly supporting local artists by exhibiting their art on the walls or giving them space to perform...if you're known as someone the community can turn to when it needs someone to sponsor a Little League team, chair a civic improvement committee, or raise money for the local hospital—now is the time to harness some of that good karma you've been spreading around all these years.

Write your customers and explain that you've tried to approach the new store from the standpoint that there's enough to go around, but they're not playing; they want to drive you out, and you need community support to stay in business. Ask not only for people to patronize you, but ask for other kinds of help: testimonials, buying scrip to generate extra cash, even outright donations. Flood the market with testimonials that not only show what you've done for them as customers, but what you've meant to the entire community. Approach reporters on your beat to do a story on you. Expose the competitor's predatory policies and show how they're selling below your wholesale cost (if that's true). Bring in your existing, nonpredatory competitors for a joint effort. And most of all, *show how you are different—and better*. Show where the dollars go—how dollars spent in your store continue to circulate locally, while dollars spent in a big chain are sucked away to a distant corporate headquarters.

All this information is out there. In my area there's even an activist, Al Norman, who has made a career out of blocking Wal-Mart and other megachains from entering a community. He spends the entire first part of his book documenting the impact these super-chains have on the existing retail environment. Then he shows, step by step, how he organized to keep Wal-Mart out of Greenfield, Massachusetts. He has gone on to consult with many towns and block superstores elsewhere. His book, and two other books about surviving near a superstore, are listed in the Resources section.[47]

If someone comes in and starts undercutting your price, it won't take much to find the weakness. One service business owner faced down a deep discounter by offering to fix the competitor's bad jobs! A little creativity can go a long way against a predatory competitor.

Consider the strategies of my client Dave Ratner, owner of three pet food stores. His flagship store shares a parking lot with a Wal-Mart—and Dave is making a new career speaking about innovative success strategies that surpass the category killers. For instance, he displayed a cheap Wal-Mart fish tank along with a sign about why he'd never sell that model because he wouldn't want to be responsible for dead fish. See more at <http://www.DaveRatner.com>.

By forcing a win–lose model on you, the competitor takes a loss—but you and your customers win, and your community wins because this approach strengthens local businesses that keep dollars circulating in the community.

In all the years I've been in business, I only came across one competitor who was hostile. I'd called him up within a few weeks of his first ads on a friendly get-acquainted call, but it was clear he had no interest in being friendly. His business lasted just about a year, while my firm has celebrated its twenty-first anniversary.

Crooks

There are two kinds of people who engage in fraudulent behavior. One kind is naïve. As a writer, I run up against this frequently: I discover an article

47. *How Wal-Mart is Destroying America (and the World) And What You Can Do About It* by Bill Quinn and *Up Against the Wal-Marts* by Don Taylor and Jeanne Smalling Archer

of mine, reprinted without credit, negotiation for reuse, or payment—but when I investigate, I find that the violator is simply ignorant. He or she does not realize that this is my property, and that I have the right to get paid for it. By treating them nicely, I convert nearly all of these into paying customers, and everybody wins.

But then there are the real crooks: the ones who write piracy software that steals affiliate commissions or banner impressions; who try to steal millions of dollars through fraudulent chain letters; who simply refuse to pay their bills or deliver the goods and services their customers paid for; who break into a store with guns pointed and demand the money; who steal identities and credit card numbers to run up big bills before they get another card number and start all over again…

If someone is deliberately trying to cheat you, there's no point in being nice. Bringing your competitors along on the success train does not extend to thieves. But the rest of you, the honest ones, who are already working together in all these other ways, can get rid of the problem faster by banding together. You can lobby, you can organize suppliers, you can inform the public, and you can press for action through the police and courts much more easily than you could if working alone.

11
Give the People What They *Want*

Years ago, Jimmy Cliff had a song called "Give the People What They Want." He was referring to politics—but it works pretty well for marketing, too. Many companies talk a good line when it comes to customer service—but how many really and truly put their words into practice—that is, how many have so thoroughly integrated customer satisfaction into their mission statement that it shapes the way they do business?

Not many—but those who do are doing quite well, thank you.

B2B Marketing Biz, which is one of a series of useful newsletters from MarketingSherpa.com, profiled a company called RentQuick.com in its August 6, 2002, issue. The company offers business equipment rentals, such as laptops and projectors, to professional speakers and other business people on the go. Although it competes with much larger, more established companies in an industry that requires expensive capital purchases, RentQuick—originally based in owner Brett Hayes's home—has been profitable since its very first month and enjoys one of the highest profit ratios in its field.

And that's because Hayes set out from the start to make his company a place that his customers enjoy doing business with. The website copy is "you-focused" (on the customer) rather than "we-focused" (on the retailer). It asks immediately, "How can we help you?"; it uses trust-building techniques (guarantee, testimonial, product photos) right on the home page, and clearly offers multiple ways to contact the company—on every single page. There is a voicemail tree, but it has only a few levels—and then human beings quickly answer the telephone. Instant messaging and e-mail also get immediate attention. And Hayes encourages his support reps to answer the customer's actual question in the first e-mail. Hayes uses these electronic communication tools to answer the easy questions, but his reps actually steer customers with more complex questions toward the telephone.

Although RentQuick is a price leader, the site doesn't emphasize low prices. Instead, the company focuses on providing an extremely positive experience at every point of interaction, of which competitive pricing is only one small part. "The mantra around here is 'build trust,'" Hayes says. That means a commitment to supply the right equipment to meet the customer's needs, on time, and in full working order, and being around to support the purchase in every way.

While several of its competitors have recently closed, RentQuick continues to grow. Its new headquarters is under construction.

We've already talked about Nordstrom and Saturn, among other companies. Now think about Dell, the computer company. Breaking almost every rule in traditional marketing of computers, Dell has specialized for years in custom-building systems to the exact specifications of its purchasers—and doing it quickly.

A client of mine, Experience Engineering, has built its business by helping its clients—including some large and familiar names, as well as many smaller firms—determine exactly why customers come to them, and deliver an optimal experience based on those preferences.

EE believes that a company's brand is not just its marketing, or even its product recognition. Rather, a company brand is built on the total perception of the customer: the way that customer feels when he or she walks in, satisfaction with both the service and the product, and how the total experience is remembered (including post-sale follow up or troubleshooting). EE attempts to anticipate and understand consumers' rational *and* emotional needs, and to set up experience management systems for its clients that enhance the customer experience—which in turn increase the customer's positive perception of the brand. EE's success is in helping its clients see the experience through their customers' eyes, and sometimes its clients find themselves moving in new directions.

Many companies claim to be driven by their customers, and claim to provide exemplary customer service. And some of them—not nearly as many as those businesses that claim they do—actually follow through and provide customer service that's good enough to produce fan mail and flowers from their customers. But this is something much deeper—anticipating the customer's wants and needs and meeting them before they're even expressed. Remember Alexander Hiam's example of the photocopier loaner program? That's the kind of thing we're talking about here. The experience of doing business with you becomes almost an organic part of the customer's own consciousness. You achieve the result through scientific study, but it feels as if it comes straight from the heart. The thing the customer most wants is there, without being put into words.

In fact, a consistent positive experience may be *the* driving factor in repeat business, and in positive word-of-mouth. As franchise businesses or company-owned locations become an ever bigger part of the retail picture, this concern is spreading to every sector. Whether the store sells books, tires, or winter coats, executives want a customer to have a positive and consistent experience in Alaska, Arizona, Alabama—or Africa.

Let's look at specific examples that will make sense of this rather abstract concept:

- A grocery chain observed that many of their customers were pregnant, set aside reserved parking spaces just for pregnant women—and made CNN news!

- A major office-supply chain discovered that its clients cared even more about being steered to the right technology than about price—and changed its advertising, store signage, and other cues to bring that message forward.

- A large car-rental company noticed that its customers had a lot of stress about returning cars in time to get through the longer security lines and reach their departure gates. By halving the return time for preferred customers and establishing experiential clues that their managers were with it and efficient (giving them headsets, for example), the company made it clear to its customers that smoothing the car return was a priority—and this company was later named Number 1 in brand loyalty across all industries.

Shopping as Experience and Entertainment

Building on EE's philosophy, let's look at the experience of shopping for a moment.

Consider what's happened to coffee. Just 20 years ago, in 99 percent of US restaurants, coffee was coffee. You had a choice of regular or decaf. And it cost 50 cents a cup, but sometimes the pot hadn't been cleaned in days.

When was the last time you bought a cup of coffee like that? Coffee has been transformed into an "experience." You choose among 20 or so different beans and roasts and grinds, sip it slowly in an elegant café, and pay $2 to $5 for the privilege. Even some highway rest stop service stations offer half a dozen gourmet blends.

Last summer, we discovered the Vermont Country Store, packed to the rafters with all sorts of exotic local foods. They give out hundreds of dollars worth of food samples every day, their parking lot is always packed, their cash registers are always ringing—and their prices are substantially higher than other stores, which more than covers the cost of all that free food. Once again, this is an example of a scenario with a lot of winners: the store, of course, which is constantly busy; the suppliers, who see substantially increased sales after people sample the merchandise; the local economy, which gets a big shot of tourist dollars and a number of jobs; and the hungry tourists, who can actually get lunch walking around sampling the food. By creating a tourist experience instead of just a place to shop, this store has found a formula to set itself apart from other food retailers.

If you create a craft or manufactured good, make your shop into a destination by showing the public exactly how your product is made. I still remember, as a child, touring the Hershey chocolate factory; the image of chocolate flowing from a huge cauldron (and the wonderful smell) is indelibly burned in my brain, even though Hershey has since replaced the real factory tour with a movie. But as a customer and as a marketer, I still love a good plant or craft studio tour. It builds a palpable connection between the user and the product, and the percentage of tour-takers who purchase something afterward is very high. In recent years, I've toured cheese plants, wineries, an ice-cream factory, glassblowers, a *damasquiña* (gold inlay) workshop in Spain, textile studios, and much more.

In recent years, shopping itself has become a tourist experience. In my own area of western Massachusetts, a company called Yankee Candle has made its vast retail complex into the largest tourist destination in two counties—with not only an enormous collection of candle shops, but also an exhibit on the history of candle-making, a Bavarian Christmas theme room, model trains running above the heads of tourists in many of the shops, eateries at every price range, etc. This store is part of a corporate headquarters complex that stretches on both sides of a town line. (The company's other outlets are simply candle shops; this one gets busloads of tourists.)

Similarly, other chains have blended shopping and entertainment. To name a few examples: Disney and Warner Brothers, Hard Rock Café, and—aimed at a very different audience—The Museum Store and Ten Thousand Villages (the latter has a charitable component that adds another benefit to the mix: helping indigenous craft artists come up out of poverty).

part three

HANDS-ON WITH COOPERATIVE, PEOPLE-CENTERED MARKETING

12

Getting Noticed in the Noise and Clutter: A Brief Introduction to Effective Marketing Techniques

In this part of the book, you'll learn how to take the principles we've been talking about and apply them in real-world marketing. Although I don't have the space for a full discussion of practical marketing here, I do want to give at least a brief summary. If you want more detail than I can give here, let me refer you to *Grassroots Marketing: Getting Noticed in a Noisy World*, my comprehensive book on how to market effectively for maximum impact at minimum cost. I've also written over five years' worth of monthly practical marketing tips, available for free online at <http://www.frugalmarketing.com> and, not surprisingly, most of the techniques in that book and in the tipsheet archive are totally suited to Marketing That Puts People First.

The reason—they work better! These strategies are cheaper, more effective, and easier to implement than the typical win-lose strategies. For instance, if your operating costs are lower, your prices can also be lower—or your service standards higher. And you may find ways to shine a spotlight on your suppliers and customers, and bring them along with your success.

Here's a checklist; if your next proposed marketing or customer service initiative meets these criteria, the chances are good that it's in harmony with the abundance mentality, and that your prospects will see your message as beneficial:

■ Incorporate top-quality customer service into every aspect of your business. Train your staff in how to greet customers in person and over the phone, how to resolve complaints and follow up to make sure they're resolved—and how to go the extra mile so the customer really feels special. Empower your workers as much as possible to satisfy customers. If you've reached out to an ethnic or subculture community, have people on hand who come out of that community, speak the language, understand the cultural context, and can make customers feel welcome. Remember how much easier and less expensive it is to get more business from an existing customer than to recruit a new customer—*if* that customer had a positive experience. But it has to be genuine; I saw a sign recently at a well-known national chain that talked about how its employees were all empowered to help—but when I called to get the wording of the sign so I could put it in this book, I was told, "I'm not allowed to give that out; please call our corporate headquarters." Worse, my wife had a mild customer service request that should have been easy for such an "empowered employee" store to accommodate. Yet the manager told us that company policy prevented him from doing what we asked, and the store lost our business as a result. In other words, the company didn't take its own message very seriously, so how could anyone else?

- Target your marketing to your exact audience—and, as much as possible, *only* your exact audience. Don't waste your money and other people's time trying to reach—and annoying—people who are not your prospects.

- Treat your prospects as intelligent, thinking, feeling people—don't ignore their emotions, but create marketing materials and campaigns that engage your prospect both intellectually and emotionally; those that only involve emotions and ignore rational thinking too often come across as patronizing, or just plain poorly thought out—while those that ignore the emotions come across as limp and boring.

- Be sensitive to the cultural nuances of your target audience. This means knowing the demographics and psychographics, using the right media to reach your particular set of prospects, and creating marketing that "sings" to the people you most want as customers. If you have a storefront in East LA, run Spanish-language radio ads on Spanish-language radio stations—and make sure every shift includes several Mexican-American employees who speak Spanish fluently. If you want to reach the deaf community, mention in print media that your event will be interpreted into ASL. If you sell luxury goods, a soft-spoken, elegant ad campaign on the local classical music station may be appropriate. If you run a feed store out in the country, sponsor a tractor pull or cow-milking contest and put notices in the local shopper or underwrite the swappers slot on an AM talk station. If you own a trendy downtown eatery, open your doors to a free 5 p.m. gourmet appetizer tasting, and publicize it by distributing fliers the previous day as commuters leave their offices. If you stock heavy metal CDs, organize a concert of local artists and get a rock station to copromote it. If you sell high-end computer processors, a multifaceted Internet campaign makes sense. If you're a deep discounter, distribute money-saving coupons on cheap newsprint.

- Be scrupulously honest in every headline, claim, or offer (more about that in the next chapter)—but still use copy that makes your audience sit up and take notice.

- Always take advantage of every honest chance to build your reputation. Turn your customers, your employees, and your competitors into evangelists for your business.

13

Honesty in Copywriting

Everybody knows you win new customers by making outrageous claims, right?

Wrong—unless, of course, they're true.

If I want my words to sell a product, that product should be strong enough to do so without tricking the buyer. I know that if I trick someone, I may make a sale—but I've lost a customer for life! Whereas if I show the merits, back up my claims, and focus on the way this product solves a problem, eases a hurt or fear, or satisfies a need, I will build that lifetime relationship.

Oh, and one more thing. I like to look in the mirror and see someone who is doing good for the world. Lies and trickery won't accomplish that! I happen to have a gift for writing, and I use that gift to make the world better. That includes being honest with myself and with my readers. My soul is not for sale!

Without tricking people, I want to capture interest—move the reader to action—and still feel good about myself in the morning.

Yes, it can be done! I do it for clients every day, and have been for more than 20 years.

There's a fine line between making something sound as good as possible and deceptive, overblown hype. Don't cross it! As many wise people have advised, underpromise and overdeliver. This strategy works pretty well in face-to-face sales, or even on the phone. If you surpass expectations, you get a very loyal customer who becomes an evangelist for your brand. In my own business, for instance, when a client submits a job and asks for an estimate of the cost and turnaround time, I generally respond with my best guess about the upper end of the possible range. Since usually it takes less time and therefore comes in cheaper, I have clients who are simply delighted.

Those who overpromise and underdeliver, however, have just sacrificed a long-term client relationship for the quick sale. And that is in fundamental conflict with the People First approach. Your customer loses because a shoddy product, or one that is inappropriate for the stated need, doesn't solve the problem and therefore was a waste of money. And you lose because all that careful buildup, all the time and expense of wooing a customer, has been wasted and you have to do it all over again. Worse yet, that unhappy customer is likely to complain to friends and colleagues—and perhaps to 10,000 of your best prospects on an Internet discussion list! [48] That kind of negative branding is really tough to overcome. So there are practical as well as moral reasons to do right by your customers!

At the same time, if you're relying on written words to make a sale, underpromising may not be enough to get the order—especially if you're using a medium that doesn't offer visual, sound, or sensual clues (for instance, text-only e-mail). Your writing alone must be persuasive. It must convince the vaguely interested thinker to become a prospect, and then turn your prospect into a living, breathing customer. So in copywriting, underpromising is not the best approach. You want to promise exactly what you can deliver, because to offer less means you might give up the sale, while to offer more leads only to disappointment and its resultant problems. And you want to move your prospect to action!

This can take some practice. I do it for my clients every working day, in a wide range of media. Here are a few basic principles of effective copywriting:

Understand Your Audience and Your Medium

If you write the same way for a press release as for a direct-mail sales letter—or use the same ad on a highbrow, low-key classical music station as on an in-your-face, loud and brassy rock or hip-hop station, your marketing will be a failure. You must know your audience and reach them with an on-target approach.

---

48. This actually happens quite frequently. For example, look what happened to Priceline.com in the Nov. 11, 2002, *I-Help Desk*. This is a moderated list, where all posts have to be approved. Find the discussion at <http://list.adventive.com/SCRIPTS/WA.EXE?A2=ind0211&L=I-HELPDESK&P=R1820>.

Here's a concrete example. We just had a four-way primary for a three-town State Representative race. One candidate took the time and trouble to individualize his campaign mailer for residents of each town, talking about the issues that were important in that specific town; he came in first, not surprisingly. Another candidate sent a very general "vote for me" letter and the sample ballot for the largest of the three towns, which happened to be his home town. I live in the smallest of those towns, and when I got his mailer, I thought, "He's surely not going to do very well here!" Of this candidate's votes, 87 percent were from his own town (where he came in first, but led the overall winner by only 16 votes). By making no effort to reach voters in the other towns with a targeted message, he assured himself of losing. In fact, he came in last in the field of four.

Focus Your Copy on Why it's to Your Prospect's Advantage to Do Business with YOU

So many marketers focus their copy on "I, me, we." Guess what—the prospect doesn't care about that! The prospect wants to know how you can do one or more of the following:

- Solve a pressing and urgent problem
- Relieve pain or fear
- Improve his or her financial condition, romantic life, or skills and knowledge
- Provide entertainment or other stimulation

I'm going to quote two brief (slightly modified) sections from the very long and extensive copywriting chapter in *Grassroots Marketing*, because I think they do a good job of summarizing this very important point:

Great Copywriting

Many experts cite the AIDA formula: Attention, Interest, Desire, Action [and one expert, Jeffrey Eisenberg of Future Now, adds an S at the end, for Satisfaction].[49] I've expanded this to ten points. Great copywriting:

1. Catches the reader's attention with something relevant;
2. Addresses the reader's fears, anxieties, and/or aspirations;
3. Stresses specific benefits to the user, not the features that lead to those benefits;

49. As quoted in Adventive's *I-Copywriting Digest*, No. 075, Nov. 11, 2002.

4. Offers to solve the reader's problem, in the most specific terms possible;

5. Provides the reader with a chance to acquire something of clear value—but only for a limited time;

6. Pulls the reader toward an immediate action step;

7. Shows the consequences of a failure to act;

8. Includes solid, substantial validation of your claim by someone else (a customer, an expert);

9. Backs up claims with comparisons to competitors and a strong guarantee; and

10. This should be obvious—provides the necessary order form, address, and/or telephone number to allow the reader to move forward.

You probably won't get all ten in every marketing document, but strive to include as many as you can. [The book goes on to explain each of these ten points in detail, with examples.]

Ogilvy's Principles

The late David Ogilvy, founder of Ogilvy & Mather, one of the world's largest and most successful ad agencies, was a believer in research. Based on extensive testing, he developed guidelines for effective ads. He scattered them throughout his book, *Ogilvy on Advertising*, and I've gathered them together:

- If five times more people read headlines than body copy, your headline must sell—or you've wasted 80 percent of your ad dollars. Promise a benefit in your headline to attract four times as many readers.

- For the same reason, mention the brand name in your headline.

- Headlines below an illustration have 10 percent higher readership than headlines above the picture—but never put the headline under the body copy.

- Caption every illustration and use sales copy in the caption. Captions have much higher readership than body copy.

- Focus the art on one person, not a group—or focus on the product.

- Keep the language simple and the copy interesting (and that lets you use long copy, which Ogilvy favors).

- Use a great lead.

- Six times as many people read editorial copy as ads. So consider making your ad look like a story. Ads that look like editorial content can get past the reader's automatic filter against advertising. Thus, full-page text-heavy ads with drop capitals [the first letter set in very large type, hanging down a few lines], serif type [the tiny feet at the edges of certain letters], black ink on a white background, set in three- or four-column type, *without* the company logo, can work very well.

- Short lines increase readership.

- Devices such as bullets, asterisks, and arrows help readers into your copy.

- Draw attention to key points with bold, italic, call-outs, bulleted or numbered lists, etc.

- If using long copy, break the page up graphically: use a two-line subhead between your headline and the body copy, start the body with a drop cap (13 percent increase in readership!), use no more than 11 words in the first paragraph, and use subheads every couple of inches. And use good leading [vertical spacing between lines]—it increases readership 12 percent.

14

Practical Tools for Effective Marketing

As I said in Chapter 12, one of the great things about Marketing That Puts People First is that it enables you to take advantage of some of my favorite low-cost, high-impact marketing tools. Here's a very brief look at how to approach traditional grassroots marketing from a win-win point of view.

Media Publicity

Coverage by the media conveys an implied endorsement by an objective, trustworthy source—something you can't buy. So I am a *big* believer in promoting through media publicity; on average, I do about 50 to 70 media interviews per year. That includes radio, print media, Internet-only media such as e-zines, and even a little television. I've been quoted in the *New York Times, Christian Science Monitor, Boston Globe, Los Angeles Times, Entrepreneur, Inc., Fortune Small Business,* Microsoft's bCentral small-business website (which just brought me another book order, over a year after the article appeared!), *Woman's Day,* and a host of two-bit media outlets you've never heard of unless you live in that community. One of those two-bit media outlets, a tiny little newsletter with just 3000 circulation, sold over 70 books for me, at full list price plus a shipping markup!

The best publicity is a home run: it builds credibility, increases your branding and visibility, draws the attention of other media, and stimulates lots of direct sales. Any marketing that can hit all four of those bases is clearly a winner. But even if all you get is first base—credibility—it's worth doing. That's all I've gotten from my mentions in the *New York Times* and others. The *Times* story, with its one-sentence quote from me, would be useless in my press kit—but my press kit can now legitimately say that the *Times* found me a worthy story source.

But what do the media get out of it? *The media need stories!* Broadcasters (in the US, at least) are required by law to provide a certain percentage of public service programming. Print media must fill a "news hole" in order to wrap content around the ads.

We've already talked about how you can bring your competitors (or colleagues in different parts of the country, or clients, suppliers, etc.) into news and feature stories by suggesting their names for a "roundup" story, where the media outlet interviews several people in a field. If you each present a different perspective, you should all get some coverage. But that's only one among many ways to get the benefits of press coverage.

If you're a good writer, consider writing and placing your own articles, or even a regular column. Many, many extremely successful marketers batch up a bunch of articles and self-syndicate to dozens of publications. In many cases, the only compensation is a detailed resource box explaining who they are, what they can do for people, and how to get in touch. Other marketers prefer to make the articles themselves into an income stream, are much more selective in the markets they penetrate, but get paid as much as a dollar a word to place their articles. Of course, they usually get a much smaller bio, and interested prospects have to track them down. Therefore, you may want to mix both approaches, as I do. I have some articles available for free reprint, with certain conditions. But if I create new content for a publication, I expect to get paid for it.

An even better trick than approaching the media cold—even if you have a great story, they are so deluged, they may miss it—is to provide useful information to journalists who are already working on relevant stories. Most of my "famous" media appearances came through a service that actually transmits information about what journalists are seeking sources for which stories; this is the secret of how a lot of publicists get ink and air time for their clients. PR firms currently pay $2700 a year to get this information; however, I have a colleague who is the service's only authorized reseller. He supplies story query feeds to individual clients for only $495 per year or $195 for three months.[50] You can read his article about how it works at <http://www.frugalmarketing.com/prleads.shtml>.

---

50. Prices are current as of December 2002.

Speaking

Meeting planners need speakers who can capture the audience's interest and impart useful information (they are *not*, however, looking for a blatant sales pitch from the podium). Again, there's a large mix of free, low-paying, and highly paid opportunities, and you can expect to spend a few years working your way up the pay ladder.

But even if you speak for free, you'll have the chance to sell informational products, to distribute handouts that include information not only about your topic but also about how you can help your prospects, and how to get in touch. And if you provide solid, useful information—especially if you can do so while entertaining your audience—you'll find that yes, prospects in the audience seek you out to consult, to buy your products, or to hire you for another speech. And, of course, the meeting planners will remember the good job you did for them, and spread your name around to others who can use you. After all, if you deliver more than an audience is expecting, that reflects favorably on the meeting planner, and on the audience's willingness to come back and pay another registration fee the next time that planner offers an event.

You'll find a number of practical tips on speaking in the back issues of my Monthly Frugal Marketing Tips, available for free at <http://www.frugalmarketing.com/marketingtips.shtml>.

Internet Discussion Groups

The Internet is so powerful that in *Grassroots Marketing*, I spend over 35,000 words—nine chapters—on it.[51] We've talked about reaching *only* your actual prospects; what makes the Internet so potent for marketers is the incredible segmentation of interest groups, and my very favorite item in the Internet marketing toolkit is participation in discussion groups.

If you're not familiar with them, these are communities of interest that come together in cyberspace, through e-mail, the Web, threaded bulletin boards and forums, or Usenet "newsgroups"—different technologies that accomplish the same thing: drawing a group of people together to talk about something they all have in common. And they are a lot of what makes the Internet special; instead of speaking to a local meeting of 20 or so people, you're in front of hundreds or even thousands of like-minded

---

51. *Grassroots Marketing* has 39 chapters and over 300 pages. It totals over 150,000 words—more than three times as much information as the roughly 45,000 words in this book.

people around the world—often including "stars" in the field, as well as people just getting their toes wet in a new interest.

No matter what topic interests you, there's bound to be a discussion group about it. These are the epitome of the People First mindset, and watching them operate since I joined my first discussion list in 1995 has helped formulate a lot of the core thinking in this book. Just at random, I tried a couple of subject areas at Topica.com, one of the major places to locate e-mail discussion groups. A search for "wine" returned eight different lists, including one for wine makers and one for fans of strawberry wine. "Fibromyalgia" returned 22 results, and "garden" yielded 200 lists.

The culture is focused around giving information, sharing success stories, asking questions to improve your products, your business, and the quality of your business thinking. People subscribe to lists that interest them, choosing by topic from literally hundreds of thousands of possibilities. From around the world, members chip in to share their expertise.

Many marketers have found that helpful participation brings them work. I've already talked about how it works for me, and how discussion list participation is actually my largest single source of new marketing clients; it's also been my largest source of paid speaking gigs. Now, a good part of why this works so well for me is that I do take the time, week after week, to answer questions and provide a lot of information. That turned out to be an amazing credibility builder in the group, and clearly motivated some of my earlier clients to try me out. Once I had satisfied a few folks, my reputation—and sales—built very quickly.

My original agenda in posting was not even to get clients, but to be consistently helpful to others, so that when I asked a question—even a really dumb or off-topic question—other people would answer it out of loyalty, because of the useful advice I'd given over time. It is definitely easier to get your questions answered if you're willing to give of yourself.

Over the years, I've provided hundreds of hours of free consulting to these lists—but I've gotten back far more than I've given out. The discussion groups I've participated in have provided me with everything from market research to new product ideas to computer technical help. Together, the list members create a resource that is more valuable than any newspaper or magazine, because it's based on the real-life experience and academic knowledge of hundreds of people out there in the trenches. Helpful advice comes from superstars in the field, who still find it useful to participate, and also from unknown people quietly succeeding in their own niche—people whose advice you would never have stumbled upon if you were looking for it on your own, because it's not in the traditional literature. List culture also creates genuine community; people start to really care about each other's successes and trials, not only in the business context, but as one human being to another. And if there's an opportunity to get together face to face, you feel as if you're meeting old friends. Even a shy person will feel as if he or she already knows a lot of people, and the interactions can shortcut a lot of the "getting to know you" stuff—because you really do know each other already.

An added benefit: since feeding articles to websites and publications is a great way to market yourself for free, or maybe even get paid, some of your best posts can be "recycled" into articles or even books, and spread around to reach new audiences.

Discussion lists exist in several different technologies; choose one that's comfortable for you. I use e-mail discussion lists, because most of them are available as a digest of all the posts for a day, which I can then print out and read easily off-screen (my eyes get tired from working at the computer all day). Other people prefer newsgroups or Web-based forums; some still use BBSs (bulletin boards) that date back to the days when services like The Well, CompuServe, and AOL weren't integrated into the Internet. Find e-mail lists at <http://www.topica.com> or <http://www.yahoogroups.com>, and find Usenet newsgroups at <http://groups.google.com> or <http://www.december.com/cmc/info/>.

User-Friendly Websites with Newsletters

Your website is another necessary (and inexpensive) arrow in your marketing quiver. The site should be quick to load, easy to navigate, and genuinely useful to your prospects, journalists, investors, and any other constituencies that might visit. If they find helpful information and a sense that they can trust you, visitors will buy from you at all hours, whether or not you're open for business or sitting at your computer.

Because most people will only visit once even if they intend to come back again, it's crucial to have a way to capture e-mail addresses: newsletter or e-zine subscriptions, notifications of events or of new content (if it's not done too often), free downloads, etc. However, if you plan to use these addresses to create a marketing relationship, explicitly ask for permission. And *never* allow anyone else access to these addresses; that's a sacred trust and you will not be forgiven if you betray it.

Also include as many ways as possible to contact you: e-mail, phone, fax, and postal (even your cell phone or pager, if you use them to be accessible to clients).

One of the many two-sided benefits in a good website is that providing visitors with the information they need reduces the administrative burden on you! If your support staff answer the same questions over and over, put up a FAQ (Frequently Asked Questions) page on your site. If you're in an industry where prices fluctuate, let visitors get price quotes dynamically, right from your website. If you distribute information, e-mail and download files can automate much of the process while saving you significant printing, mailing, and labor costs. And of course, if people need to contact you, get your hours, locate your nearest distributor, find a map to your store, the website makes it very easy. Even as far back as 1995, Sun Microsystems' Neil Knox estimated that his company saved about $8 million annually by using the Web—not even counting a substantial direct-sales benefit.[52]

Because the novelty has long since worn off, it's no longer enough to simply say, "visit my website." All your publicity and marketing should not only list your Web address, but also provide at least one specific reason to visit. Here's a real-life example of how that can create a benefit: I did a radio interview in Kansas City about my book on Frugal Fun. I always give reasons to visit the site, such as "I mention a number of great cheap airfare sites in back issues of my Frugal Fun Tips. You'll find them on the archives page at www.frugalfun.com, in the travel section." A listener heard the interview, went to the site, ordered both the fun book and one of the marketing books, and then hired me for quite a bit of copywriting.

It's well worth the effort. On the Web, you have essentially unlimited space to convince prospects to enter into a relationship with you. A well-designed, content-focused website can become one of the best and most cost-effective marketing tools you can create, and one that can keep evolving as your business and the online culture change over time.[53]

52. *WebMaster*, Nov./Dec. 1995.
53. It doesn't have to be difficult, either. See the Resources section for a tool that easily and inexpensively creates and hosts clued-in websites that generate significant traffic.

Apparel and Premiums

Everyone loves a new article of clothing; why not do something up that reinforces your brand? You get exposure for your message, and your prospect, customer, or trade-show visitor gets something spiffy to wear. But don't just slap your name and logo across a T-shirt. Crystallize your core message into a few words that attract attention and provide a reason why someone viewing the shirt (hat, tote bag, etc.) would want to do business with you—and include your URL, nice and big. For shirts, forget about the golf shirts with a tiny logo under the pocket. The whole idea is to be seen by people encountering the person wearing your shirt. For the same reason, print on the front side; in the winter, the back will be covered up by a warmer layer.

If the clothing is attractive enough, people may want to buy it from you. That's good, because it means they'll actually use the item. You can also give them away as incentives for buying certain quantities, etc.

As for other advertising specialties, in general, I don't think most of them are all that effective. But if you can come up with something that dovetails well with your products and services and that can actually reinforce your brand, it's worth a bit of experimentation. Refrigerator magnets are one possibility; I know my refrigerator is full of them, holding up all sorts of temporarily important notes. And yes, I do look at the names and services. Another would be something so useful that it won't be ignored, and so closely identified with your business that it serves as a constant reminder of what you can do for the client. A coffee roaster could do mugs, or even an imprinted carafe—but wouldn't want to do a calendar. A CPA—or a renewable-energy consultant—might want to give away solar calculators. An auto parts store could use auto sunshades—nice, visible canvas, that! (Print on both sides, since they're reversible.)

Highly Targeted Advertising, Direct Mail, and Telephone Sales

Though they're relatively expensive compared to the other tools in our toolbox, there is a place for traditional advertising methods—both online and offline—and for direct mail. Purchased ad strategies that may make sense over the Internet include advertising in e-zines and newsletters that match your demographic target, purchasing clicks (but *not* exposures) at search engines—and perhaps, in very particular circumstances, banners or other types of display ads. Offline, highly targeted ad buys such as trade journals and Yellow Pages, or deeply discounted (but still targeted) ad buys such as remaindered space may make some sense.

One key is to make sure that you have targeted so carefully that the vast majority of people seeing or hearing the ad, or receiving the letter, will be actual prospects (your own customer list is a very good place to start). Often, classifieds can be a better bet than display ads; they target even within the publication's readership, and they're a lot cheaper.

And the other key is to provide copy that focuses on what the reader or listener wants, and not on what you want. Solve problems, relieve pain, demonstrate benefits—and reinforce in every part of the ad or letter how your mutual success philosophy is going to create a better situation for the prospect.

These two keys will move your advertising into "everyone wins mode": the people you talk to will be eager to hear from you, and you'll slash your marketing costs by not talking to people who are not your prospects.

In any medium, test your ad on a small audience before rolling out a big, expensive ad buy.

Finally, remember that unless you've hit the prospect who has an immediate and crucial need, one impression is generally not enough. So consider a telephone follow-up program—but train your telephone sales staff so thoroughly in customer-focused marketing that the calls are actually welcomed. (Quite a bit of detail appears in the telemarketing chapter of *Grassroots Marketing*.)

Guerrilla Gifting

It's long been known that giving something away can be very good for business. I'm not going to talk about the obvious ways, such as free gift with purchase or annual holiday gifts, or giving away obsolete inventory with a marketing piece about the latest version. Rather, let me discuss a few unusual, innovative marketing tricks that offer long-term benefit to your business, and to the recipient.

LIBRARY GIFTS WITH BOOKPLATE OR STAMP:

I wish I could take credit for this brilliant idea, which comes from a reader who prefers to remain anonymous. The beauty of it is that any business can benefit by using books as a guerrilla marketing weapon—whether or not your business has anything at all to do with books.

Here's the deal: look for holes in a library's collection. Buy a few books to fill those gaps—and there are a gazillion ways to find cheap books. Now, put a bookplate or rubber stamp on the inside front cover, and perhaps a few other spots: "Donated By (your business name, marketing tagline, URL, and contact info)." Obviously, the more closely the books match the interests of your own prospects, the more value you get out of it.

Still, even if it's not such a close match, there can be substantial benefit—especially if there's a strong cross-cultural component, which makes the materials exotic and desirable.

My correspondent writes about how he used this to help the owner of a specialized training school.

> I bought several books when I was in Spain, in Spanish, of direct interest to high school students, put "donated by xxx school" with a rubber stamp at least 10 times per book, on the title page, back page, on blank pages in the text, and sent them to the high school Spanish teacher in the town where my friend lives. Spanish books? For a Spanish teacher? Books that can't be bought at any price in the US, mostly, but which cost me 1–5 Euros in Spain? The teachers will use them until the paper crumbles. Those advertisements will last 20 years at least. Tourist posters are free in Spain—stamp your "donated by ..." on them, and send them to high school Spanish departments, I assure you your ad will be on the wall until the paper falls apart.[54]

He also bought a case of my 1993 book, *Marketing Without Megabucks*, at a deep discount, and plans to distribute them (mailing by ultra-cheap International M-Bag, with each box marked as M-Bag postage paid in case the tags get separated), to libraries in Spain, India, and elsewhere—again, as a gift from a business he wishes to benefit. "Libraries abroad are *desperate* for good books in English. Even if it's an old book, those books will be on the shelf for decades."

He has been using this little trick for a decade now, and has noticed definite and positive results.

---

54. Personal e-mail to me (Oct. 31, 2002). Used with permission.

WORK WITH YOUR RETAILERS AND SALES OUTLETS TO BROADEN THE SALE:

A retail partner will be very happy with you if you significantly increase the total sale, even if that means plugging products that don't come from you. Kare Anderson, whose *Say It Better* e-zine has been brightening my e-box for years, shows how to make the cash register numbers jump at an author appearance:

> Gain more in-bookstore visibility by helping bookstore managers increase sales. When seeking book-signing opportunities, offer to provide a 20-minute mini-seminar. Busy people will attend; you inspire them to tarry. In advance, provide a camera-ready tip-sheet and seminar announcement that booksellers can print 2-up on an 8 1/2" x 11" sheet. In it include "the companion collection" of three books you recommend reading, in conjunction with yours. If possible refer to a local author you admire. In the seminar, refer to those books as you discuss yours. Suggest that the bookseller display your book, and "the collection," on a special table, along with a Lucite stand to hold your tip sheets—and build buzz for your event. Also provide 2- to 3-sentence mini-reviews of the books you recommend (include your name and book title at the end) and provide these mini-reviews in printed form for booksellers to tape to the shelves where those books are displayed.[55]

This costs you nothing but a few minutes of your time, yet leaves the retailer with a long-term appreciation that you have his or her needs at heart. That will create word-of-mouth buzz for you long after your celebrity appearance is a distant memory.

A spin on this strategy, for authors particularly, is to review books by others at Amazon.com and other book review sites. Of course, your review will mention that you're the author of such-and-such a book that readers of this book will also enjoy.

There are literally hundreds of ways to bring others along and pump up overall sales. We've talked earlier about bundling items from different companies, and about working out partnerships for premiums and incentives, which you can either purchase or obtain for free. Then there are

---

55. Kare Anderson, writing in *SpeakerNet News*, Nov. 1, 2002. Used with permission.

package stuffers, where you find people whose products complement yours, and insert fliers for each other's products into outbound shipments. If utility companies can do it, why can't we?

Many food manufacturers have teams of people who go to supermarkets and do cooking demos and product samplings; it doesn't take a genius to figure out that this will usually create a sharp spike in sales—and, with luck, some long-term converts. Think about how this model can apply to your business, even if you don't sell food.

We've mentioned going after co-op ad programs if you are a retailer. If you're the manufacturer or distributor, consider sponsoring a co-op program (but understand the laws). And it doesn't have to be just advertising, either; for instance, offer co-op dollars toward your retailers' direct-mail and Web campaigns, too—but insist on approving the copy before you put your name on the marketing piece or provide any funds. In fact, because so few businesses understand effective marketing, you may want to offer co-op dollars only if you supply the creative elements (copy and design).

DONATE YOUR PRODUCT TO A STORE:

Go to the store manager and offer to donate some special, collectible version of your product. Examples: For authors or musicians, a couple of signed copies of your latest book or CD; for manufacturers, a one-off prototype; for food manufacturers, a low-volume run made with some unusual seasonal ingredient. Get a written agreement to buy more through regular channels if they sell within a certain time. The store then gets more than double its usual share of the price, can place the goods in inventory and track them, and has an incentive to display your wares prominently. By making the store owner, manager, and staff into allies and evangelists, you help them while gaining significant exposure for your merchandise; they'll likely sell your products with a good deal more enthusiasm.

DONATE YOUR PRODUCT AS A PREMIUM:

Here's another brief excerpt (rewritten slightly, for clarity out of context) from *Grassroots Marketing: Getting Noticed in a Noisy World* about giving away your products and services on radio and TV. (The paragraph about Roosevelt Best is not in the original.)

Both commercial and noncommercial broadcasters give away amazing numbers of records, concert tickets, retail gift certificates, and other prizes;

these are almost invariably donated by publicity-seeking merchants. Prizes may be raffled off in charity auctions, given to random callers or those who can answer trivia questions, or used as incentives for people to subscribe to noncommercial stations. (Charity auction premiums may even yield the added bonus of a line in newspapers or brochures listing your prize and the time it will be auctioned).

If you listen, you'll hear a rap on the order of "I have a hot tub pass for two at Heavenly Heat on Bath Street in Anytown for the third caller who can tell me Ringo Starr's kid brother's name" or, at subscription time, "Jeff Jacobs, who owns the Witty Words bookstore, just called to offer a twenty-dollar gift certificate to the next two people who pledge thirty dollars or more. So if your library's getting kind of run-down, now's the time to call in your subscription."

Not only do you get the air time, but when the lucky winner comes to redeem the prize, s/he will have to make the acquaintance of your business or service—and, ideally, be added to your valued regular customers. Meanwhile, the station gets more money. Everyone wins.

Virtually all prizes and premiums given away by commercial stations are bartered for publicity. Often, it's possible to barter goods and services directly for advertising [discussed in more detail in *Grassroots Marketing*, Chapter 13].

And here's a different twist on that: Roosevelt Best, of Naturally First, a London-based nutritional supplement company, approaches magazines to offer a freebie to their readers in exchange for space to sell his own products. While it's common to offer a freebie and then upsell through your own literature when you fill the order, this is a bit different, because not only does it happen at the same time as the original exposure, but it doesn't cost Best anything for the space. He runs full-page ads, of which the top fourth is devoted to the freebie; the rest is his to use as he wishes.[56]

Better yet, get someone else to spring for "your" cost. Jordi Herold of the Iron Horse Music Hall is a master at this.[57] "Whenever possible, you get somebody else to pay for the premium you're using. If we use tapes, CDs, posters, a weekend at an inn, somebody else has paid for all those things." Herold even manages to get subsidized ticket giveaways. "Often, when we

56. Best has been a client, but I read about this in Karon Thackston's *Business Essentials* e-zine, Nov. 20, 2002 <http://www.ktamarketing.com>.

57. The Iron Horse is a nightclub in Northampton, Mass.; Herold, a very savvy marketer, is cited as a source in many sections of *Grassroots Marketing*.

use tickets as premiums, we are able to get the record companies to pay for them. They buy a block of tickets." Herold has also taken risks to promote unknown bands; the groups' record companies will buy enough seats to pay the performers, and have Herold give all the rest of the tickets away for free. Free sampling is a time-honored marketing method—and then, of course, a number of the attendees will buy CDs and pay to see future shows.

Here's a variation from Guerrilla Marketing author Jay Conrad Levinson:

> If you advertise on a show that's built around an on-air personality, give the announcer a freebie: lessons, product samples, a dinner in your restaurant, whatever. Then just provide your radio celebrity with an outline of what you want covered in your ad. The radio star may provide you with an eloquent, unsolicited on-air testimonial that may run far longer than the number of seconds you're actually paying for.

I don't talk about it in *Grassroots Marketing*, but there are obviously many ways to benefit by giving products away besides ensuring media coverage. For instance, whenever I go to a Chamber of Commerce networking event, I bring a copy of one of my books to give away as a door prize. If there are a hundred people in attendance, a hundred people get to see my book waved around and hear my name mentioned. Similarly, I donate copies to many charity fundraisers.

ACHIEVEMENT, BIRTHDAY, AND ANNIVERSARY GIFTS

Forget drowning in the deluge of holiday gifts and cards; recognize your customers at other times. If you become aware of some significant achievement (or a personal milestone such as a new baby or a marriage), send a congratulatory note and perhaps a small gift. If you collect information in a database, send a gift for your client's birthday, or on surpassing a certain purchase level—ideally, a gift that fits in perfectly with the kinds of things that that customer likes to buy. Your more creative approach will be noticed and appreciated. My client Dave Ratner, who owns several pet food stores, buys Thanksgiving pies for over a thousand of his best customers, whom he tracks with a barcode-scannable club membership, just as many supermarkets do.

The Triangle of Expertise: Get Paid to Do Your Own Marketing

Marketing does *not* have to be a cost. It can be revenue-neutral, and it can even be a profit center.

Lately, I've become especially enamored of what I call "the triangle of expertise." In my case, I do some of my best marketing via speaking, consulting, and writing/publishing, all of which support each other, and all of which can be *revenue generators*. (If you prefer to add media visibility for a "rectangle of expertise," that's fine too—except that I've never found a way to be paid for getting interviewed by a journalist. However, publishing your own articles in various media can be a very definite income stream.)

So, when I do a speaking engagement, I am getting paid to speak. I will sell some quantity of books to attenders, at full price or slight discount. Two or three of the one hundred or so attenders will probably hire me to write some copy for them. And of course, the person who hired me usually knows of me either because of reading one of my books or through my participation in a publishing discussion list, which came about because I write books.

People buy my book and then hire me to write for them, or people hear me speak and buy my book, or they hire me and decide to learn more about copywriting and marketing, so they buy the book. Or people who know of me through media exposure (including Internet discussion groups, e-zines, and my own and others' websites, as well as print, radio, and TV) know and respect my advice on copywriting, so they buy the book to gain more of it.

I don't have a monopoly on this. Use your book (audio, video, etc.—some kind of tangible information product) and consulting credentials to get speaking gigs, sell your books after the talk, and follow up—as soon as you get back to your office —with the consulting prospects who eagerly, desperately, press their business cards into your hand (annotate them before you stick them in a pocket!).

Martha Retallick, owner of LRP Designs in Tucson, Ariz., points out that you can draw the triangle differently depending on your own set of skills and interests. In her case, she doesn't make paid speeches—but her Web design services complete the triangle.

15

Marketing as Social Change, and Social Change as Marketing

One definition of marketing is an action or message (or series of actions or messages) that causes someone else to take an action of some kind: to buy a product, try a service, accept a new idea. In short, marketing involves persuasion.

The best persuaders, the best negotiators, have always come from a mindset where both parties win.

They tend to be excellent listeners, able to tune in exactly on the other person's issues, whether or not those issues are verbally expressed. And they are able, time and time again, to figure out how the other person can benefit from what they want to happen—and not just benefit, but actually meet—or even exceed—his or her goals. Sometimes this is a matter of persuading…sometimes, listening—and responding with ideas that move everyone forward.

My earliest training in marketing was in doing public and media outreach for various social change groups I was involved with as a volunteer. And I still live my life around the idea that I *can* make a difference in the world I live in—that I have both the skills and the obligation to try to make the world better in some way. And I believe there's tremendous synergy between marketing and social change. Social change groups that ignore marketing will find themselves unable to reach anything more than a marginal splinter of an audience; their ideas will never become mainstream because there is no one to interpret their message for the mainstream audience. And when a social change message becomes mainstream, that's when the ideas take hold and the change begins to occur. Social change advocates who make no attempt to reach the everyday world are just spitting in the wind. It may feel good, but it won't accomplish much.

Indeed, some of the most "out there" social change folks were marketing geniuses, understanding fully and completely how to play on the edges of mass consciousness and instill radical changes: Abbie Hoffman and Jerry Rubin of the Yippies, Dan and Phil Berrigan and their group of radical Catholic pacifists, Martin Luther King, Jr., and Saul Alinsky, to name a few prominent examples from the 1960s. In our own generation, the Adbusters collective clearly understands and uses the medium it attacks.

And it's not just a left-wing thing, either. The rise of the New Right in the 1980s was directly related to its understanding of marketing...from Ronald Reagan's successful presidential campaigns to televangelists like Jerry Falwell who understood the enormous power the medium provided, to Rush Limbaugh and other conservative talk-show hosts, to Newt Gingrich's brilliantly crafted message of a Contract With America. The marketing mavens on the Left, incidentally, quickly dubbed that last one the "Contract ON America," in the underworld hitman sense.

These are people who have changed the direction of an entire society, from the shift against the Vietnam War and the acceptance of the Civil Rights movement to the abandonment of the safety net 20 years ago. They did it by combining the persuasive power of top-notch marketing with the ability to organize vast numbers of people. And the best organizers understand that the line between marketing and organizing is blurry, and that they need to walk both sides of it.

These skills are learned. Even Martin Luther King, Jr., was not a natural-born marketer; his early sermons were less than thrilling. His biographer, Stephen B. Oates, noted the evolution:

> His sermons tended to be sober and intellectual, like a classroom lecture. But he came to understand the emotional role of the Negro church, to realize how much black folk needed this precious sanctuary to vent their frustrations and let themselves go. And so he let himself go. The first "Amen!" from his congregation would set him to "whooping" with some old-fashioned fireworks, in which he made his

intellectual points with dazzling oratory. For what was good preaching if not "a mixture of emotion and intellect"?[58]

By the time he made his "I Have a Dream" speech, King had become fully aware of the marketing power of what he did, and of the impact he could have on a national and international audience. Of 86 sentences in the speech, 82 use classic marketing techniques of storytelling, analogy, and metaphor—that works out to 95.35 percent. This was the oration named the best speech of the twentieth century,[59] beating out Roosevelt's "Day of Infamy" and Kennedy's "Ask Not What Your Country Can Do for You," among others. This was the oration that catalyzed a nation to do something about ending segregation once and for all—and ensured King's own place in history—and it was a marketing document!

This chapter focuses more on the marketing of ideas than on the marketing of products or services. Maybe you can think about how visionary thinking can relate to success with marketing tangible items, or services, in your own business.

Barbara Waugh, Corporate Revolutionary

I stumbled on a book recently called *The Soul in the Computer: The Story of a Corporate Revolutionary*, by Barbara Waugh.[60] She recounts a number of amazing stories in her career at Hewlett-Packard, where time after time, she was able to gain consent from her higher-ups to do socially conscious projects that computer companies don't usually get involved with. And interestingly, not only did she continue to get the company involved, but each time, after the dust settled, she had more responsibility and a bigger paycheck. Her initiatives not only accomplished many of their missions, but kept getting her promoted.

Barbara Waugh epitomizes the power of positive persuasion. In the book's foreword, Alan Webber of *Fast Company* magazine comments about people who will change your life:

They do it by rearranging your sense of what is possible... convincing you that the only limits to your future are those

58. Stephen B. Oates, *Let the Trumpet Sound: The Life of Martin Luther King, Jr.* (New York: Plume, 1983), p. 56.
59. *Baltimore Sun* article, quoted in the *Daily Hampshire Gazette* (Northampton, Mass., Jan. 15, 2001, p.1).
60. *The Soul in the Computer: The Story of a Corporate Revolutionary* (Makawa, Hawaii: Inner Ocean Publishing, 2001).

you…impose upon yourself…by expressing the absolute conviction that you have within you dreams and aspirations that you've never acknowledged—and…the absolute confidence that your dreams matter absolutely.…It wasn't that Barbara is a great talker, and that what she said changed my life—quite the opposite. It was that Barbara is a great listener, and how she listened changed my life.

Coming out of volunteer work in the civil rights and women's movements, Waugh was originally hired by HP in 1984 as a recruiting manager for a manufacturing division, charged with hiring 110 new engineers. And she wasn't there very long before she began to work for small increments of change within the company. Her strategy was to do what's right and stand up for it, move slowly enough to maintain support but quickly enough to galvanize people, find "coconspirators" who would support her within the struggle, and then find ways to change "enemies" into allies within the corporate structure. One of her first victories was in confronting an arrogant, belligerent colleague who didn't even realize he was intimidating most of his co-workers; he not only changed his behavior but became an important ally.

Scaling up these steps, she took on ever-bigger projects. Over time, she initiated a corporate-wide sustainability drive, started a focus group of women in technology that evolved into a series of national conferences, and eventually helped create a massive program to bring HP's technology to developing countries where it could play a major role in empowering the local populations—the aim is to serve the world's poorest 4 billion people in ways that can help bring them out of poverty and still turn a profit for the company. These are only a few of her projects over the years.

The whole focus in her odyssey is the idea that doing well is a natural consequence of doing good: make the world better, and you will be more likely to succeed personally and professionally—and the company you work for will benefit as well.

In fact, in every interview I've read with the world's most successful entrepreneurs, nearly all of them talk about some sort of higher purpose. They didn't generally start their businesses just to make a lot of money—but to accomplish a much larger social goal. Perhaps this is why even some of the corporate giants who came out of the "robber baron" period of the late nineteenth and early twentieth century were driven to massive philanthropy. To name one example among many, steel magnate Andrew Carnegie funded hundreds of small-town libraries, in villages that had never had a library before.

But Waugh was not a company founder or CEO. In fact, after I shared a draft of this section with her, she wrote:

> I wish we could somehow draw attention to the enormous uncelebrated, unidentified entrepreneurial initiative of the grassroots—it isn't only or even mostly CEOs, but you'd never know it from the literature—perhaps due to the business model of consulting—the function that most amplifies what's going on inside companies—that requires the big bucks that only the top can cough up. I've advocated, with limited success, that a percent of consulting dollars spent by the top on the top be made available to the rest of the organization, as an internal consulting budget for the troops.

As I read Barbara's book, what strikes me first is her amazing power to persuade others—because she goes about it in a systematic way, seeking alliances and stakeholders, and clearly showing at every corner that all the players come out ahead.

The second thing that strikes me is her willingness to examine herself critically, to push herself past her prejudices. Many times in her career, she finds that someone she expected to be hostile to her ideas was actually a key ally—but first she had to overcome her initial resistance to even starting the conversation.

And the third thing that struck me is the parallel between her story and my own story. I too came up out of various social justice movements and had to learn how to work with mainstream people, how to be open rather than cynically skeptical, and how to accomplish change from within the power structure as well as outside of it. While I haven't changed the direction of a major corporation, I've had a few important victories, and they give my life purpose.

Case Study: Save the Mountain

Here's an example that I'm particularly proud of. In November 1999, a local developer announced a plan to desecrate ridgetop land abutting a state park by building 40 trophy homes. The original newspaper article interviewed several local conservationists who basically expressed variations on "Oh, this is terrible, but there's nothing we can do." I said, "Oh, yes, there's something we can do!" The article appeared on a Friday night. By Tuesday, I had drawn up a petition, posted a Web page, called a meeting for two weeks later, and sent out press releases and fliers about the formation of "Save the Mountain."

Note that all of these actions are marketing actions. I could have called a meeting and not told the public, and then a few friends of mine would have shown up and realized that we couldn't do very much. But by harnessing the power of the press, the Internet, and the photocopier, and crafting a message that would resonate with my neighbors—that not only was this terrible, but that there *was* something we could do—I was able to spark something that truly had an impact.

I expected 20 or so people to come to the first meeting; we had over 70! From that day until December 2000, we fought the project on every conceivable level: technical issues like hydrology, rare species, and slope of the road...organizing and marketing pieces including a petition drive (over 3000 signed), turnout of up to 450 at various public hearings, lawn signs, tabling, a big press campaign with over 70 articles...working with the state Department of Environmental Management to investigate options for saving the land...

Literally hundreds of people got involved with some degree of active participation. Many, many people brought widely varying expertise to the movement, far more than any of us could have had on our own.

By using my own skills in marketing and organizing, I was able to harness the outrage and despair and shock that were felt throughout our valley when this project was announced and turn it into a powerful—and highly visible—public force. As a group, we had about 35 core activists, and all of us were working on many levels, both public and private. The persuasion in this case was not about the desirability of stopping the project; we had near-consensus on that, community-wide! But the persuasion piece focused on the ability of a committed group of people to make a difference even when the experts said it was impossible.

And make a difference we did! Within two months of starting the campaign, we had established ourselves firmly in the public eye as a can-do organization, a force to be reckoned with—and we had actually shifted the discourse from "There's nothing you can do" to "Which of the dozens of ways we can pursue will be most effective in stopping this development and making it impossible for someone else to despoil this land in the future?" Collectively, we had used our powers of persuasion, and our skills at reaching the public with our message, to change blocking the project from a pipe dream to an inevitable result of our actions.

As it turned out, a wealthy benefactor stepped forward, publicly stated that she was inspired by our efforts, and wrote the state a check to buy and preserve the land. The state took title in December 2000. We were delighted, since we had fully expected to spend five years contesting permits and so forth. Meanwhile, our group had gone on to organize a regional summit of all the parties with interest in the region's two mountain ranges, including governments of several cities and towns. The proposed bylaws that came out of that effort were adopted by one town and are being considered by the others—and the town that I live in actually passed several new protective laws while the battle was still going on—because we organized for them. You can read more about all this at <http://www.savemtholyokerange.com>.

You probably have victories in your own life as well, where you achieved a marketing success (using "marketing" in a broad sense, not just to sell a product). If you're inspired to share them, I'll consider putting your comments on a Web page with reader contributions on persuasive and ethical marketing.

Please mail your success stories to me at shel@principledprofits. com with the subject: Persuasive Marketing Success Story. <mailto: shel@principledprofits.com?subject=PersuasiveMarketingSuccessStory>

16

Community-Focused and Charity/Social Change Marketing

The Save the Mountain story that ends the last chapter is the perfect segue to one of my favorite parts of the marketing toolbox: affinity marketing that benefits both you and a worthy cause.

In my other marketing books, I demonstrate that working with a charity allows you take advantage of free media publicity and many other marketing opportunities that are denied to strictly-for-profit enterprises. Newspapers promote your event, radio stations have you on the air to talk about it, store owners let you put posters in their windows, libraries make space for your flier on their bulletin boards—and lots of people show up, you have a great event, and present the charity with a large check.

Of course, when you give back to the community, the community is eager to partner with you. You gain valuable credibility and PR as a socially minded company, and attract that segment of the market that values social responsibility. Combine this approach with superior products and services, and you're almost unbeatable.

Think about companies like the original Ben & Jerry's;[61] the company's willingness to donate 7.5 percent of pretax profits to social causes, its socially conscious purchasing and employment practices, environmentally friendly manufacturing methods, and counterculture marketing strategies helped justify its premium prices. Ben & Jerry's has over 40 percent of the superpremium ice-cream market; its plant is Vermont's single largest tourist attraction.[62]

---

61. I am referring specifically to the company as it existed before it was bought by Unilever. I am not familiar with its social goals since the buyout.
62. B&J's internal strategic marketing document, prepared by Stratego Marketing, Inc., was found in a Google search at <http://webpages.shepherd.edu/ARAISOVI/Ben%20&%20Jerry's.ppt>.

Charity tie-ins are also a great way to change slow times into busy times. An in-store benefit event during a normally slow period can create great foot traffic. As it happens, I'm writing this section on the fourteenth annual "Piece of the Pie Day" in my area of western Massachusetts. Restaurants donate 10 percent of gross revenues for the day to a local food pantry, and all the participating eateries are mobbed. This year, 175 restaurants from four counties are participating; there were about 40 the first year. Obviously, this event works for everyone involved.

The possibilities range from quick, easy events that raise a small amount of money to elaborate affairs requiring months of planning. Just to provide some idea starters, here are a few possibilities:

- Invite cookbook authors or famous chefs to do dinner fundraisers
- Auction or raffle off artwork, memorabilia, or other exotic prizes
- Donate a percentage of sales to a deserving charity
- Volunteer for a dunking booth at the fair, to benefit a local agency
- Organize or participate in a bike-athon, skate-athon, dance-athon, etc.
- Sponsor a Little League team

Here's the truth: people *want* to do the right thing! If you provide a social benefit and your offerings are otherwise comparable with those that don't offer the same benefit, you will find a niche.

Many, many companies have done extremely well for themselves by being socially responsible, and then telling others about it. We've already mentioned Ben & Jerry's. They may be the most well publicized among companies that act out of social responsibility, but there are hundreds, if not thousands, of others. A few examples: Seventh Generation (environmentally friendly products), Stonyfield Farm (supports community-based farming), Co-op America (worker-owned businesses and consumer co-ops), ShoreBank (funds businesses started by low-income people), Malden Mills (the owner kept everyone on payroll after a disastrous fire closed the plant for several months—and the national publicity he received propelled him into a professional speaking career, in his 70s)...

17
The Beauty of Barter

One way of making sure everyone feels like a winner is to keep cash out of the deal entirely. Whether you call it a barter, swap, horse trade, or exchange, everybody wins on a good trade deal. If you're trading your own products and services, you're getting the deal for your wholesale cost. Better still, if you can barter something you bought but don't need anymore, you're trading your junk for someone else's treasure.[63]

Here's an easy example: It's often possible to barter any advertising purchase—if you have something the media outlet wants. If you write an article, for instance, you can sometimes get the editor to throw in a free ad (in addition to a good-sized resource box at the end of the article). Barter might also work if you sell a product the organization needs, such as office supplies or health insurance.

Multimillionaire publisher and copywriter Jeffrey Lant gets all his ads through barter. "The last time I bought an ad was a long time ago. You do a lot of creative swapping. Most people do not have a swap track in their brains—they expect to pay cash for everything. I'll try to get something on a swap first before I ever pay cash for it. I've gotten art, gems, foreign travel, air tickets, liquor, lots of books, (as well as) an enormous amount of media space."

What does he trade? His marketing advice column, space in his direct mail postcard deck and/or his catalog, books, consulting time, and, of course, his vast mailing list. "Names are a kind of currency. As you develop a mailing list, a lot of people want those names. Names will get you free cards, ad space, a better spot in a [post]card deck, other names."

If you build your business as a speaker (paid or volunteer), that opens

---

63. Much of this chapter is taken from my earlier book *Grassroots Marketing: Getting Noticed in a Noisy World*—but some new material has been added.

up many barter possibilities, too. Here are a few examples, and the names of the speakers who suggested them:[64]

- When speaking at a conference that also includes a trade show, offer an extra session on a different topic for free, in exchange for booth space. (Elizabeth Fried)
- Speaking for free to a local chapter of a national organization? Prepare a contract that clearly states the dollar value of the gift, and trade for a complete list of attenders (with contact information) as well as a recommendation and contact person at the national office. (Padi Selwyn)
- If there's a local nonprofit group related to the topic of your talk, get volunteers from that group to staff your sales table, in exchange for giving the group space to display and sell its own wares (Bob Ingram)

Sometimes, because of the difference in production cost and market value, barter can help leverage an enormous amount of marketing clout. Here's how it worked for another speaker, Tom Antion <http://www.antion.com>:

> I was asked to speak at the first Wharton Business School Club e-commerce event in Washington, DC. I provided 100 of my Multimedia Internet Marketing Training CDs as "sign up premiums." They cost me $2.00 each to duplicate, but at a retail cost of $199.00 it made me a $20,000.00 sponsor. My name was plastered on many of their promotions around the world to both the public and Wharton School Graduates.[65]

What can you supply to a publication, broadcast station, or professional conference? Among many possibilities: computer equipment or software; food or lodging; office equipment; travel; temporary office staff; video production; website design and maintenance; landscaping; furnishings, decorations, and houseplants; pest control; bookkeeping; professional services (from accounting to zebra-striping); writing and illustration; messenger services; indexing; subscription processing; circulation and distribution (either of a publication or of promotional materials); premi-

---

64. All of these examples are taken from *Speaking Successfully: 1001 Tips for Thriving in the Speaking Business*, 1999 ed., edited by Ken Braly and Rebecca Morgan from tips that originally appeared in their *SpeakerNet News* e-zine. Order online at <http://www.speakernetnews.com>.

65. Personal e-mail from Tom Antion (Dec. 8, 2002) as a side comment when I asked him for a blurb. Used with permission.

ums and advertising specialties; books and records; free tickets to events; contracting; office cleaning and maintenance.

Keep in mind, too, that you can also barter something the media outlet can give away to its own audience

You can probably find three or four things you can offer in trade. When you hear of a new magazine, newsletter, radio station, or other ad venue, be particularly assertive in suggesting barter; new media outlets are frequently undercapitalized, and often have long wish lists. Newsletters of nonprofit organizations are also usually quite receptive to the idea, for the same reason.

Complex Barters

A one-for-one trade is simple to arrange, but sometimes you need to go an extra step. For example, say you paint houses and you want to barter painting for advertising slots on a radio station. The station doesn't want painting, but the ad manager is complaining about high dental bills. You paint a dentist's office, the dentist fixes the ad manager's teeth, and the radio station gives you air time.

Finally, consider a formal barter exchange network. You pay an annual fee, plus a percentage on everything you "buy" through the network. You accumulate credits as people use your service or acquire your product, and you subtract them as you patronize others. National barter associations always have plenty of advertising available for trade dollars; evaluate each offer as you would any other media buy.

Non-Advertising Barters

Of course, you can barter for many goods and services other than advertising; I've focused on ad barters here simply because advertising is a part of marketing, and this book is about marketing. But the same principles work for any product or business service you need. I've bartered my copywriting skills for an array of items: a significant discount on painting my house, massage and chiropractic, a large and elegant hand-woven 100 percent wool Persian rug, a composter for our yard. The only factors that limit the extent of barter are your imagination and your ability to find willing barter partners. For the latter, it's just a matter of figuring out who would benefit by what you offer, and how to approach them so they see the benefit to their own business. (Note: Barter is taxable, but should usually zero out.)

18

Taking the Concept Beyond Marketing: Abundance and Sustainability in Businesses and in Society

You may find this chapter a bit off topic—but to me, it's the most important chapter in the book. This is where you may find yourself ready and willing to make an enormous difference in the larger society. By the time you've read this chapter, I hope I will have motivated you to do something to bring these ideas out of the marketing realm, and into the world at large.

It's probably worth an entire book, and I may write that book sometime down the road.

I ask you to bear with me and read it through, even if you think it doesn't pertain to you.

A Recap of Our Core Principles

Time for a quick review: let's just remind ourselves of some of the most important principles in this book, all in one place.

- Ethical marketing—based on quality, integrity, and honesty—not only *feels* better, but *works* better

- The more people who have a vested interest in your success, the more likely that success becomes—and thus, marketing that benefits your customers, employees, suppliers, distribution/retail channels, and even competitors is a key to that success

- Cooperation is an extremely effective strategy

- In the abundance paradigm, there's plenty to go around—and in the vast majority of cases, that means "market share" is irrelevant

- When you've set up the right marketing systems, selling becomes less of a concern—because by the time a prospect contacts you, that prospect really *wants* to become your customer

▤ To achieve your goals, you can follow numerous paths; rarely is there only one way to accomplish your agenda

Now, let's keep those principles in mind as we start to look at the big picture: the whole huge canvas of Planet Earth.

What Could a Sustainable Future Look Like?

What kind of world would we live in if the abundance paradigm were integrated into every aspect of society? There'd be enough to go around, yes—enough food, shelter, energy, drinkable water, medical care, and so forth. But what kinds of changes would that create?

Take a few minutes to think about that, and jot down your answers. (You can e-mail them to me if you like: shel@principledprofits.com, subject line: Sustainable Future Ideas <mailto:shel@principledprofits.com?subject =SustainableFutureIdeas>; I'll consider them for posting on a Web page dedicated to this topic and perhaps "immortalize" you in a future book.)

Here is the short version of my vision (writing from my perspective as a resident of the United States):

By eliminating scarcity, we eliminate poverty and famine. Everyone has adequate food and water for survival, and, as that frees up time that had been spent on basic survival, people who have never had the "luxury" of education begin to build new skills and knowledge. A massive but noncoercive educational campaign not only raises the literacy rate, but lowers overpopulation worldwide—when we're talking about sustainability, that means keeping the world sustainable for future generations, too. And the drastic reduction in population growth will actually find support among the affected populations, because they will realize that nearly all of their children will live; therefore, they do not have to have so many babies just to make sure there is someone to take care of them in their old age.

By switching the entire society from nonrenewable to renewable, clean, abundant energy—solar, hydrogen, wind, water, etc.—we eliminate oil, coal, and uranium as reasons to go to war. We also eliminate the stranglehold that certain foreign governments have on us—and can deal with them on the merits of their actions, and not out of a need to appease or overpower them in order to maintain access to their oil. Pollution will be drastically decreased, and as a result, the cost of medical care will go down. Reforestation programs will make sure that we have not only adequate timber resources, but adequate oxygen supplies, for generations to come.

The energy shift includes switching agriculture from chemically dominated factory farming to methods that not only preserve—even enhance—the soil, but produce significantly healthier and more nutritious food. Over time, this will raise yields, eliminate another source of pollution, and again reduce medical costs. These organic farms will produce in abundance, and the challenge will be distribution: getting food to the parts of the world where, so far, there hasn't been enough to go around. And food production won't be limited to farms. City dwellers will grow food (and collect solar energy) on their rooftops and windowsills. Most families will have access to at least a small garden.

Transportation and housing planning will lead many communities toward a village cluster model, where the buildings are relatively close together and the open space surrounding homes and workplaces is available to all. There will be a movement away from commuting long distances; many more people will either work from home or within bicycling distance.

Throughout every aspect of society, systems will be designed along the lines of John Kremer's biological model. Changes in building and transportation design will allow all of us to live more lightly on the earth, while enjoying greater physical comfort.

The communications revolution will continue; the Internet will reach into the remotest villages. This will open up vast powerhouses of learning, sustainable commerce, and global community building; every home becomes its own university campus. And that, in turn, will eventually lead to locally based, grassroots mass citizen action to bring down dictatorships around the world. And this awesome, globally-distributed computer power will be able to automate a lot of the drudge work of managing corporations, schools, hospitals, and factories.

With no need to wage war for resources, and most dictators removed from power by their own citizens, the need for such a vast and powerful military apparatus will be sharply reduced. The enormous resources the military currently consumes can be channeled toward such pursuits as environmental regeneration, research to cure diseases, and perhaps even a nonmilitary exploration of space. Terrorist groups will have far fewer reasons to attack us, as these policy changes shift us away from behaviors they see as oppressive (e.g., consuming far more than our share of resources, propping up vicious dictatorships, and sanctioning exploitative labor practices abroad).

The economy will undergo some major shifts. As some of society's largest entities shrink and retract, the abundance mentality will make sure these people are not unemployed. There will be a movement toward a shorter workweek; instead of 40 hours on the job (and up to 10 more hours commuting), most people might work 20 hours or so, and would be able to maintain or expand their standard of living at that level (because so much less of their paychecks would be spent on consumption of nonrenewable resources). This, in turn, could lead to a major flowering of arts, culture, science, recreation, volunteering at service agencies and schools, and lifelong learning

Hmmmm. I think I like this new world! May I go and live there?

Making it Happen

So…how do we get from where we are to the kind of world you came up with, or the kind that I described?

For starters, we need to recognize that a lot of the ideas and technologies in that vision are already here today. We just need to alter their distribution so they're accessible to all. Here's a quick and easy example: millions of computers are replaced every year, and most of them are in fine working order. A computer that's three years old may not be able to run the latest software, but the word-processing, spreadsheet, Internet, and other applications that it *can* run would make a huge difference in the lives of people who have no computer.

So instead of creating a solid waste disposal problem and adding it to the landfill, you could donate that computer to an inner-city minority youth program, or to a college in a developing country. Years later, when it has truly worn out, materials recycling programs can take it apart and use the raw materials to make new computers—but first, computer repair training programs could use it to provide hands-on experience.

In every aspect of our lives, these changes are possible and practical.

I'm going to conclude this chapter by excerpting two articles from the Sustainable Business section of my webzine, *Down to Business*: notes on speeches by two of today's greatest "practical futurists": Amory Lovins and John Todd.[66] As you read, think not only how such changes could impact your own business, but how this harmonizes so well with John Kremer's concept of "biological marketing," which we discussed earlier. Once again, the earth can show us how to do amazing things with minimal resources.

Amory Lovins: Reinventing Human Enterprise for Sustainability

Amory Lovins is a sweeping visionary in the tradition of Leonardo da Vinci, Ben Franklin, and Buckminster Fuller—but his focus is on how humans can fit better into this earth of ours. Though he lives in the Colorado Rockies, where it often goes well below zero Fahrenheit (-18°C) on winter nights, his house has no furnace (or air conditioner, for that matter)—and it stays so warm inside that he actually grows bananas. He uses about $5 per month in electricity for his home needs (not counting his home office). Whether your company is looking for a huge competitive advantage, a more responsible way to do business, or both, the Lovins approach may be the answer.

Lovins built his luxurious 4000-square-foot home/office in 1983, to demonstrate that a truly energy-efficient house is no more expensive to build than the traditional energy hog—and far cheaper and healthier to run.

The payback for energy efficiency designs in Lovins's sprawling, super-insulated home was just 10 months. The sun provides 95 percent of the lighting and virtually all the heating and cooling, as part of an ecosystem of plants, water storage devices, and even the radiant heat of the workers in his office.

Noting that energy-efficiency improvements since 1975 are already meeting 40 percent of US power needs, Lovins claims a well-designed office building can save 80–90 percent of a traditional office building's energy consumption.

Conventional building logic, claims Lovins, says you insulate only enough to pay back the savings in heating costs. But Lovins points out

---

66. Both speeches were given to the E. F. Schumacher Society <http://www.smallisbeautiful.org> in Amherst, Mass., Oct. 27, 2001. You'll find the complete articles, along with several other good pieces, available for free in the Sustainable Business section of Down to Business magazine <http://www.frugalmarketing.com/dtb/dtb.shtml>, as well as hundreds of articles on smart marketing and entrepreneurship in other sections of the magazine.

that if you insulate so well that you don't need a furnace or air conditioner, the payback is far greater, "because you also save their capital cost— which conventional engineering design calculations, oddly, don't count."

"Big savings can cost less than small savings," Lovins says—*if* designers learn to think about the overall system, and how different pieces can work together to create something far greater than the sum of its parts. The trick is to look for technologies that provide multiple benefits, rather than merely solving one problem. For instance, a single arch in Lovins's home serves 12 different structural, energy, and aesthetic functions.

He consulted on a 1656-square-foot tract house in Davis, California, where temperatures can reach 113 degrees Fahrenheit, which does not need any heat or air conditioning. If the methods used in the house were introduced on a mass scale, construction cost would be $1800 cheaper than a comparable conventional house, and maintenance costs would be cut by $1600 per year. While it's easier to achieve these dramatic savings in new construction, even on a retrofit, the savings can self-fund these improvements.

Just by switching an industrial project from long, narrow, turning pipes to short, wide, straight pipes, Lovins was able to cut energy costs by 92 percent—and slash construction and maintenance costs and operating noise, too.

Lovins has also looked long and hard at transportation. He and his associates have developed amazing car designs, under the service mark Hypercar.^{SM}

Again, it's a whole-systems approach. By changing everything from the construction materials to the power source to the aerodynamics to the possible uses of a parked car, Lovins's team designed an SUV that not only can hold a whole family (or two people and their kayaks), but weighs 52 percent less than a Lexus SUV, can go 55 miles per hour on the energy the Lexus uses just for air conditioning, achieves the equivalent of 99 miles per gallon (except that it runs on hydrogen fuel cells—330 miles on 7.5 pounds of hydrogen), offers greater safety than a heavy steel SUV (even if it hits one), is undamaged by a 6-mph collision, emits only water, and is so well made that its designers expect to offer a 200,000 mile warranty!

When parked, the Hypercar vehicle "could be designed to become a power plant on wheels"; plug it into the electrical grid and watch your meter spin backwards, eliminating any need for nuclear or coal plants.

Lovins says cars like this could be in production within five years, dominate the market within a decade, and essentially wipe out today's steel-bodied internal combustion-fired, polluting cars within 20 years. (Hypercar, Inc., spun off from Lovins's Rocky Mountain Institute as a separate business in 1999.)

But for Lovins, even this is not the true big picture. "We still have to look systemically at land use, alternative modes, virtual mobility, and transit; we need to drive less or run out of roads and space." Even a super-advanced car can still get stuck in traffic, after all.

Lovins has developed a few key principles over the years:

- Design whole systems for multiple benefits, rather than components for single benefits
- Redesign production to close all the loops in a system and eliminate both waste and toxicity
- Reward service providers and customers who do more and better, with less, for longer
- Reinvest the resulting profits in scarce natural and human capital

The sustainability model can have a huge impact not only in developed countries, but in areas of severe poverty, too.

Lovins described an effort by the Zero Emissions Research Initiative to "grow" houses out of bamboo in a developing country with an acute housing shortage. The houses cost only about $1700 each, can be located where they're most needed, and can finance themselves by selling excess bamboo to "carbon brokers" for energy or other uses. And of course, if the bamboo is cut back (rather than cut down) to build the houses, the plant can regenerate and maintain an ongoing income stream.

Curitiba, Brazil, was a struggling city with deep-rooted problems. But when city planners began to look at its needs as a system, they were able to shape the agenda and pull the city out of crisis. A few examples: Rather than building superhighways, they increased road capacity along several parallel routes; this was both much less costly and far less destructive to the neighborhoods. Then they provided density bonuses so that the arteries best suited to large traffic volumes could support more residents. And then they reinvented mass transit, with a bus system that moves people as efficiently as a subway, but at a fraction of the cost. The fully integrated approach to changing from a dying to a thriving city is told in the book, *Natural Capitalism*—and can be read online at <http://www.natcap.org/images/other/NCchapter14.pdf>.

Using nature as a model and mentor, Lovins encourages companies to rethink their waste streams, too. In many cases, the waste of one system can be "nutrient" for another process. Closing these loops is both cleaner and more efficient. (See the next section, on John Todd, for more on creative reuse).

One of the great things about the Lovins approach is that it relies on the private sector to "do well by doing good," as the Quakers say. Companies that adapt to the systemic approach will be highly profitable key players in the new economy. "Early adopters will enjoy a *huge* competitive advantage," Lovins says.

John Todd: "Waste Streams" into "Fish Food"

In downtown Burlington and South Burlington, Vermont, you'll find a very unusual industrial park: a place where brewery wastes turn into a growing environment for mushrooms—and in the process create an enjoyable biopark, a green and vibrant ecosystem in the middle of the business district, where downtown workers can enjoy a unique natural setting.

Welcome to the Intervale, 700 acres of sustainable enterprises and ecofriendly public spaces.

This project is one of many lasting gifts to the earth—*and* to the business world—from John Todd. Todd defines ecological design as "the intelligence of nature applied to human needs": a new partnership between the ecological needs of the planet and the physical and commercial needs of human beings that can "reduce negative human impact by 90 percent."

Todd described a project in Cape Cod to save a pond that was receiving 30 million gallons of toxic landfill waste a year. His staff remineralized the pond by adding a rock floor and brought the dead bottom water up to get light with floating windmills. They installed "restorers": solar and wind-powered biosystems that process the contaminated water through a series of cells, each with different ecologies—integrated networks of microorganisms, higher plants, snails, and fish. Each of these mini-ecosystems removes specific toxins from the water. Designed to work as a system, the restorers—nine cells in this case—digested 25 inches of sediment within two years—and the water is clean enough to drink now. "This pond was constipated; we uncorked it," says Todd.

In Maryland, Todd worked on a project to clean up waste from a large chicken-processing plant. The highly concentrated waste was being dumped into a lagoon, which flowed directly into Chesapeake Bay. "We planted restorers with 28,000 different species of higher plants and animals. It grew very quickly. Each was designed to break down or sequester different compounds. We reduced the electrical power to convert the waste by 80 percent and cut capital costs in half." This kind of system is "very effective in agriculture, because it's cost-effective enough for farm use."

One of the underlying principles in this work is sharing resources among different pieces of the system and changing the paradigm about what's left over. Instead of disposing of a waste stream, Todd encourages people to think about how to use that material as an input. The goal is zero emissions: no waste generation at all. If wastes are considered as inputs, they can lead to new commercial enterprises—for instance, a mushroom farm. All of a sudden, the cost of waste disposal turns into capital for a new revenue stream (kind of like getting paid to do your own marketing—see page 125.)

This is how the natural world works, at least when undisturbed by human pollution. When these systems are integrated together, they not only eliminate waste, but also provide shared synergy, reduce costs, spread technical and legal expertise, and create both economic and environmental improvements—as occurred at the Intervale, where biowastes feed a commercial fish farm that also cleans the water, and the waste heat from a wood-fired power plant is recaptured to heat the complex.

These concepts can also work easily in developing countries. Todd is working on a water treatment sustainability project in a refugee camp, using a long transparent pipe to expand and contract gases. The range of temperatures and conditions is so great that it kills viruses. "I begin to see a model for college and urban food production. We can begin to think of strengthening our own food security in these troubled times. We're creating a new culture based on earth stewardship."

Todd notes, "The biotech industry looks for magic bullets—single solutions to complex problems. Nature is a symphony"; it doesn't work that way.

How Will These Visionary Thinkers Improve *Your* Business?

It is interesting to me, though not surprising, that both Lovins and Todd focus their social change work through the business community. Their innovations are not in a vacuum, but designed quite consciously to make a profit. They have found a way to integrate profound social change into a traditional capitalist business—as have Barbara Waugh, John Kremer, Bob Burg, and countless others.

And this model of sweeping social change within the business context has the power to change the world. If their stories can inspire you to create a business whose ultimate purpose is a significant betterment of the world, then I've done a very good job with this book. I hope that many of you will write to me and tell me how you've put the ideas in this book—not just the last couple of chapters—into practice. Perhaps I'll be able to gather so many success stories that I can write a sequel, sharing your successes with the world.

You'll find my contact information in the Clued-In Copywriters part of the resource section.

May you be inspired, ethical, and successful, may you find deep satisfaction in the work you do, and may you never lack for abundance in your life.

Shel Horowitz
Hadley, MA
USA
January 17, 2003

19
Resources

This is not intended to be a complete list, but a jumping-off place for further exploration; the world of information about marketing, ethics, and sustainability is indeed abundant. And although I have read a number of the books on this list, I haven't read all of them. Some just looked useful in a fairly quick glance. And some, like Tim Sanders's and Barbara Waugh's books, I not only read all the way through, but immediately started recommending to others.

I've tried as much as possible to avoid repeating information from the extensive resources list in *Grassroots Marketing*, other than Jacques Werth's book, which I felt I had to include here because I cite it specifically several times in the text.

A few of the resources here are affiliate links; every one of those is for a product that I believe in and endorse. I believe the affiliate model, properly understood, is a very powerful way to market products through the endorsement of others who truly believe in them. While it may be misused by some who throw up a lot of affiliate links without any familiarity with the product, those marketers who value their reputations will only lend their brand to superior offerings.

If you feel *this book* is a superior offering, and you'd like information on marketing it to your own audience through a commission arrangement, please contact me at:
<mailto:shel@principledprofits.com?subject=PrincipledProfitResellerProgram>.
Discounted bulk sales are also available.
Write to me at:
<mailto:shel@principledprofits.com?subject=PrincipledProfitBulkSales>.

Books

Bishop, Patrick, and Jennifer Bishop. *Money Tree Marketing* (New York: Amacom, 2001). A brilliant book, but written from the scarcity-cutthroat competitor mentality. Look at the tactics to see which ones transfer well to the People First approach, and discard anything that rubs you wrong ethically.

Blanchard, Ken, and Sheldon Bowles. *Raving Fans* (New York: William Morrow, 1993). Lessons about turning customers into evangelists, told, in the Blanchard tradition, in parable form.

Brandenburger, Adam M., and Barry J. Nalebuff. *Co-opetition* (New York: Currency Doubleday, 1996). An early book on building alliances with competing and complementary businesses.

Burg, Bob. *Winning Without Intimidation* <http://hop.clickbank.net/?frugalmar.bb0184>. Bob has been one of the people who has helped me to see the wisdom of Marketing That Puts People First. In every issue of his free newsletter, you'll see how his low-key, nonconfrontational approach leads to increased sales and a happier life. The above link will take you to the purchase page for an e-book that assembles much of his wisdom. You'll also want to subscribe to his weekly newsletter, for free, which you can do at <http://www.burg.com>.

Everett, Melissa. *Making a Living While Making a Difference: The Expanded Guide to Creating Careers with a Conscience* (Gabriola Island, British Columbia: New Society Publishers, 1999). How activists can find careers (or start businesses) that fit in well with their values and beliefs.

Evoy, Ken. *Make Your Site Sell* <http://frugalfun.sitesell.com/myss/>. Ken Evoy always jams a tremendous amount of information into his e-books. This one is actually a series of e-books totaling about 2000 pages, covering how to develop a website that focuses on what the customer needs, and then turn that focus into sales. He has several other useful e-books, and tons of free information, as well.

Fox, Loren. *Enron: The Rise and Fall* (New York: John Wiley, 2003). What happens when the world catches up to crooked companies.

Freiberg, Kevin, and Jackie Freiberg. *Nuts! Southwest Airlines' Crazy Recipe for Business and Personal Success* (New York: Broadway Books, 1998). Inside story of a company that "gets it."

Harder, David. *The Truth About Work: Making a Life and a Living* (Deerfield Beach, Fla.: Health Communications, Inc., 1997). Interviews with famous and unknown people who have passion for their work. Talks about issues such as support, cooperation, quality, loyalty, and more.

Hawken, Paul, Amory Lovins, and L. Hunter Lovins. *Natural Capitalism: Creating the Next Industrial Revolution* (New York: Little, Brown, 2002). Includes the Curitiba story and much more.

Holliday, Charles O., Stephan Schmidheiny, and Philip Watts. *Walking the Talk: The Business Case for Sustainable Development* (San Francisco: World Business Council for Sustainable Development/Berrett-Koehler, 2002). The chairmen of Dupont, Anova Holding AG, and Royal Dutch Shell's board of directors explain why sustainability is good for big business. Somewhat technical, but a perspective you don't often see.

Horowitz, Shel. *Grassroots Marketing: Getting Noticed in a Noisy World* (White River Junction, Vt.: Chelsea Green, 2000). 306 pages of practical, hands-on, low-cost marketing advice. Available directly from the author at http://www.frugalmarketing.com, 800-683-WORD / 413-586-2388.

Kelly, Marjorie. *The Divine Right of Capital* (San Francisco: Berrett-Koehler, 2001.) A compelling argument that capital, which doesn't have much to do with investing directly into corporations, is inappropriately driving the economy; corporations need to answer to their employees, and not to their shareholders (who, in general, purchase previously owned shares from other stockholders, rather than directly investing in the company.) By the editor of *Business Ethics* magazine.

Levine, Stewart. *The Book of Agreement* (San Francisco: Berrett-Koehler, 2002). If this book didn't already exist, I'd want it as the next book in this series. Levine, a lawyer, writes in his preface that 15 years ago, he "shifted… from an adversarial orientation of 'How can I win by protecting my client more than you protect your client?' to the idea of 'How can everyone get the results they desire from this collaboration?'" Very much in harmony with the ideas in these pages.

Lundin, Dr. Stephen, Harry Paul, and John Christensen. *Fish! A Remarkable Way to Boost Morale and Improve Results* (New York: Hyperion, 2000). How empowered employees, real customer relationships, and a great sense of humor turned an ordinary fish market into a magical place to work.

Lundin, Dr. Stephen, Harry Paul, and John Christensen, with Philip Stroud. *Fish! Tales: Bite-sized Stories, Unlimited Possibilities* (New York: Hyperion, 2002). Applying the Fish! principles to other businesses.

Norman, Al. *Slam-Dunking Wal-Mart.* (Atlantic City: Raphel Marketing, 1999). How to block predatory megastores.

Prashad, Vijay. *Fat Cats and Running Dogs: The Enron Stage of Capitalism* (Monroe, Maine: Common Courage Press, 2002). A harsh look at some of the corporate scandals that have rocked the business world.

Quinn, Bill. *How Wal-Mart Is Destroying America (and the World) and What You Can Do about It* (Berkeley: Ten Speed Press, 2000). Another book on the retail giant's predatory practices against not only other retailers but consumers.

Roddick, Anita. *Business As Unusual: The Journey of Anita Roddick and The Body Shop* (London: Thorsons/Harper Collins, 2000). The founder of a hugely successful socially conscious business tells her story.

Sanders, Tim. *Love Is the Killer App: How to Win Business and Influence Friends*(New York: Crown Business/Random House, 2002). A high-level Yahoo exec discusses compassion, abundance, and love as a business success tool. Young and hip, and very in tune with my views.

Tannen, Deborah. *The Argument Culture: Moving from Debate to Dialogue* (New York: Random House, 1998). The well-known gender communication expert looks at how to listen to each other and talk so as to be heard.

Taylor, Don, and Jeanne Smalling Archer. *Up Against the Wal-Marts: How Your Business Can Prosper in the Shadow of the Retail Giants* (New York: Amacom, 1994). How to thrive when a predator opens next door.

Wallace, Aubrey. *Green Means* (San Francisco: KQED Books, 1994). Profiles of environmental activists making a difference—and a living

Walters, Jamie S. *Big Vision, Small Business: 4 Keys to Success Without Growing Big: Do Well, Do Good, Stay Small* (San Francisco: Berrett-Koehler, 2002). A refreshing antidote to the idea that businesses have to become huge in order to make it. Extensive discussion of the need to build genuine relationships in business.

Waugh, Barbara. *The Soul in the Computer: The Story of a Corporate Revolutionary* (Makawa, Hawaii: Inner Ocean Publishing, 2001). Her memoir of the incredible changes she sparked within Hewlett-Packard.

Werth, Jacques, and Nicholas E. Ruben. *High Probability Selling* (Newtown, Penn.: Abba Publishing, 1996). Goes into far more depth than I can here about the selling model of doing business with those who want, need, and can afford your product.

Wreden, Nick. *Fusion Branding: How to Forge Your Brand for the Future* (Atlanta: Accountability Press, 2002). Shows how brands, in the post-mass-market economy, need to be about a great deal more than awareness. Urges companies to develop "a long-term profitable bond between an offering and the purchaser. This relationship is based on trust and loyalty, backed by everyday operational excellence and measured by customer equity."

Magazines

Business Ethics: Just what it says—for fifteen years. Great website, too: <http://www.business-ethics.com/>.

Utne: Consistently puts out a vision of sustainability, by reprinting articles and news briefs from literally thousands of obscure but excellent publications around the world. Also a huge online community at <http://www.utne.com>. "Utne" is the magazine founder's last name.

Websites/E-zines

<http://www.adventive.com/cgi-bin/a.pl?adventiv&1058> Adventive's excellent series of discussion lists probably embody the win-win, cooperative spirit better than any similar organization on the Net.

I regularly read and participate in *I-Sales*, *I-PR*, *I-HelpDesk*, and *I-Strategy*; there are several others.

<http://www.bsr.org> Business for Social Responsibility. The group's White Paper on socially responsible marketing, which I've cited several times, is located at <http://www.bsr.org/BSRResources/WhitePaperDetail.cfm?Doc umentID=269>. This document includes a comprehensive list of business organizations that ask their members to conform to a social responsibility code of behavior.

<http://www.daveratner.com> Dave Ratner speaks on how to stay competitive in the face of retail giants like Wal-Mart.

<http://www.expeng.com> Experience Engineering, which helps companies discover why their customers actually come to do business, and how they can make that experience as rewarding as possible for the customer.

<http://www.frugalmarketing.com> My own hands-on site, filled with practical tips on how to implement better, more cost-effective marketing strategies. Counting *Down to Business* magazine, the archive of my Monthly Frugal Marketing Tips, and a page of marketing articles, there are well over 250 articles on marketing, entrepreneurship, and sustainability. Also contains excerpts from my book *Grassroots Marketing: Getting Noticed in a Noisy World*. The complete articles on Amory Lovins and John Todd are here; they go into far more depth than the excerpts included in this book.

<http://www.marketingbestpractices.com> David Frey's newsletter site. Although David hasn't tried to brand himself, as (for instance) Dan Kennedy and Mark Joyner have, he consistently puts out a thorough analysis and a fresh slant.

<http://www.marketingsherpa.com> A series of e-mail newsletters and articles covering innovative marketing techniques, both on and offline.

<http://www.oceanarts.org> Ocean Arts International—John Todd's water pollution think tank.

<http://www.principledprofits.com> (principledprofit.com should bring you to the same site) The site to support and grow the ideas of this book.

Reader contributions relevant to the book will be posted here as they come in. Also the place to sign up for my free monthly e-newsletter, *Positive Power of Principled Profit*.

<http://www.sayitbetter.com> Kare Anderson's site on better communications. Kare is the author of several books, including *Walk Your Talk: Grow Your Business Faster through Successful Cross-Promotional Partnerships* and *Resolving Conflict Sooner*.

<http://www.smallisbeautiful.org> E. F. Schumacher Society website on sustainability.

<http://www.speakernetnews.com> An excellent weekly e-zine with great tips for speakers, almost entirely produced by its readers. Offers useful tele-classes and other resources, too.

WEBSITES COVERING AMORY LOVINS'S WORK

<http://www.rmi.org> Rocky Mountain Institute, his think tank.

<http://www.natcap.org/> Natural Capitalism discusses Lovins's four sustainability principles; the Curitiba story is found at <http://www.natcap.org/images/other/NCchapter14.pdf>.

<http://www.hypercar.com> Hypercar.

<http://www.pge.com/003_save_energy/003c_edu_train/pec/info_re-sourcecmml_res_proj.shtml> Pacific Gas & Electric Advanced Customer Technology Test for Maximum Efficiency (energy-efficient tract house).

<http://www.zeri.org> Zero Emissions Research Initiative (bamboo houses)

Tools and Resources to Get Publicity

ONE-STOP TOOLKIT TO CREATE AND HOST SITES THAT GET FOUND BY SEARCH ENGINES:

Ken Evoy's Site Build It! is an astonishing website creation/hosting/positioning package that sets up a successful website and e-zine. For a new site, it will save you a lot of time, trouble, and money. (I used it for the site for this book, even though I've already built three sites the old fashioned way.) Readers of this book can download a free trial at <http://frugalfun.sitesell.com/freetrial/>.

Clued-in Copywriters (In Alphabetical Order)

Note: The precondition to being listed here was to name at least one other recommended marketer. Thus, I am not personally familiar with some of these people. Before hiring any copywriter (or other communications professional), read testimonials and samples, understand the pricing structure, and make sure the writer is a good fit for the assignment. I am listed here alphabetically, with all the rest of them.

Following the general list, you'll find a small listing of book publicity specialists.

Most offer informative free e-newsletters. Read several issues and you'll have a pretty good sense of each individual copywriter's philosophy and style.

GENERAL COPYWRITERS

Bob Bly
rwbly@bly.com   tel: 201-385-1220
http://www.bly.com
Country/Time Zone: US/Eastern
"I do whatever it takes to maximize results (e.g., leaders, orders, trials, demos) at the lowest possible marketing cost. I understand not only the product but also the 'core buying complex' of the prospects—their fears, concerns, needs, wants, desires, hopes, dreams, and problems."
Specialization: Twenty years of experience in business-to-business, high-tech, Internet, industrial, and direct marketing.

Michel (Mike) Fortin
The Success Doctor, Inc.
michel@successdoctor.com   tel: 613-748-1624
http://successdoctor.com/
Country/Time Zone: Canada/Eastern
"My goal is to energize my clients' sales message in order to help turn their businesses into powerful magnets."
Specialization: Direct response and sales-letter copywriting (Web, direct mail, and e-mail marketing campaigns).

David Garfinkel
Overnight Marketing

garfinkel@aol.com   tel: 415-564-4475
http://www.davidgarfinkel.com
Country/Time Zone: US/Pacific
"Tell the truth in the most intriguing way, and you will get not only the best response, but the highest level of customer satisfaction. The biggest problem most people have with advertising is that promises are made that are later not fulfilled, and you can avoid this problem entirely by telling the truth—but in a way that *sells*."
Specialization: (1) Writing websites to sell information products online (e-books, seminars, teleclasses, software) and (2) Positioning and lead generation for outstanding individuals and successful small service businesses selling high-end, unique products.

Geoffrey Heard
MarketNOW with Geoffrey Heard
grow@marketnow.com.au   tel: +61 3 9583 0788
http:/www.marketnow.com.au
Country/Time Zone Australia/Eastern
"I aim to help you win a place on customers' mental menus and win sales through integrated, multi-faceted, and persistent communications, painting pictures in customers' minds of the benefits you offer and walking them through the steps to fulfillment. I write for every medium."

Shel Horowitz
Accurate Writing & More
shel@principledprofits.com   tel: 413-586-2388 / 800-683-WORD
http://www.frugalmarketing.com
Country/Time Zone: US/Eastern
"Affordable, effective marketing materials and strategies that get attention, online *and* offline. I find the news behind your story and make it appealing—to reporters *and* the public. I make the world *insist* on knowing why *you're* special."
Specialization: News releases/press releases, media pitch letters, Web pages, direct-mail, print ads (including classifieds), brochures, newsletters.

Robert Lerose, Copywriter/Consultant
RobertLerose@compuserve.com   tel: 516-486-0472

Country/Time Zone: US/Eastern

"Copywriting is the craft of persuasion by channeling a specific need, want or desire to your product."

Specialization: Direct mail packages, ads and brochures for business-to-business, consumer and nonprofit mailers.

Joe Nicassio
Rapid Results Marketing
joe@rapidresultsmarketing.com   tel: 562-961-3976
http://www.rapidresultsmarketing.com
Country/Time Zone: US/Pacific

"Every company has a unique, special, valuable story. When I write copy, my goal is to make your offer irresistible to your target market. Once that story is articulated in a compelling fashion, you can use it *everywhere*—your brochures, the Web, yellow pages, radio, cable TV, *everywhere!* That is why it is so valuable and critical to invest in your message development."

Kevin Nunley
kevin@drnunley.com   tel: 801-328-9006
http://drnunley.com
Country/Time Zone: US/Mountain

"We write quality sales letters, ads, press releases, and website copy at low cost with quick turnaround. The goal is to give every small business the best marketing and PR at a price that fits their budget."

B.L. Ochman
BLOchman@whatsnextonline.com   tel: 212-369-8312
http://www.whatsnextonline.com
Country/Time Zone: US/Eastern

"I call my approach Reality PR™. Most companies are still using tired old techniques—like the traditional press release—to try to draw attention to their business. I write copy for a host of new marketing and publicity outlets that are at least as powerful as traditional media."

Specialization: Web content, Reality PR™ press releases and pitch letters, newsletters, e-books, by-lined and ghostwritten articles.

Carol Page
Carol Page Communications

carol@carolpage.com   tel: 617-625-8657
Country/Time Zone: US/Eastern
"Smart, clear copy that communicates the client's story/news/product is essential. My goal is to always be sensitive to the wishes of the client, but also to the needs of the audience, whether it's the media, a client or customer, or anyone else."
Specialization: Press releases and press kits, speeches, articles, proposals, and various marketing peripherals.

Alan Rosenspan
Alan Rosenspan & Associates
arosenspan@aol.com   tel: 617-559-0999
www.alanrosenspan.com
Country/Time Zone: US/Eastern
"My approach is to write simply, persuasively and convincingly. I believe the most important word in the English language is 'you.' My goal is results. Please see '7 Rules for Direct Marketers' article on my website."
Specialization: Direct marketing, direct mail, e-marketing.

Scott T. Smith
Copywriting.Net
admin@copywriting.net   tel: 406-585-0181 / 800-798-4471
http://www.copywriting.net
Country/Time Zone: US/Mountain
"The Web is a direct response medium, and a properly written website is one of the most effective lead generators ever devised. Use Copywriting.Net to double or triple the number of new leads and customers you generate each month—without increasing your marketing budget."
Specialization: writing direct response website copy and e-mail marketing campaigns.

Joan Stewart
The Publicity Hound
jstewart@publicityhound.com   tel: 262-284-7451
http://www.publicityhound.com
Country/Time Zone: US/Central
"I don't write news releases. Rather, I train people on how to write things

such as releases, pitch letters to the media, op-ed columns, how-to articles, etc., so that they can stand on their own two feet without me."

Karon Thackston
KT & Associates Marketing
karon@ktamarketing.com   tel: 803-438-4088
http://www.ktamarketing.com
Country/Time Zone: US/Eastern
"Most buying decisions are emotional...your ad copy should be, too! KT & Associates specializes in targeted copy designed to speak specifically to your customer, search engine optimized website copywriting, and press releases."

Keith Thirgood
Capstone Communications Group
mtmmp@capstonecomm.com   tel: 905-472-2330
http://www.capstonecomm.com
Country/Time Zone: Canada/Eastern
"I believe that people make buying decisions based on emotion, and then they justify their decisions with logic. My writing reflects this by revealing the benefits of a product or service in a manner that touches the target audience's emotions."
Specialization: Websites, direct mail, brochures, advertising.

Joe Vitale
Hypnotic Marketing, Inc.
joe@mrfire.com   tel: 512-847-3414
http://www.mrfire.com
country/Time Zone: US/Central
"I write enthusiastic sales letters and news releases designed to grab attention, hold it, and lead it to action. I believe in very heart-based copywriting where sincerity takes top priority."
Specialization: Sales letters and news releases

Debbie Weil
WordBiz Report
dweil@wordbiz.com   tel: 202-364-5705
http://www.wordbiz.com & http://www.wordbizreport.com

Country/Time Zone US/Eastern

"As the publisher of WordBiz Report, I focus on online copywriting and content for e-mail, e-newsletters and the Web. I take short copywriting assignments to review and rewrite promotional e-mails, craft online text ads or to create a content formula for an e-newsletter. I also do phone consulting if you want to run your e-newsletter or email program by a tough critic. Call me."

Simon Young
Simon Young Writers Ltd
sy@simonyoung.co.nz   tel: 649-836-3331
http://www.simonyoung.co.nz
Country/Time Zone: New Zealand/UTC/GMT + 12hrs

"More than ever, business credibility is crucial. The best way to achieve credibility is to tell your story truthfully and compellingly. Copywriting is people communicating with people."

Marcia Yudkin
Creative Ways
marcia@yudkin.com   tel: 617-266-1613
http://www.yudkin.com
Country/Time Zone: US/Eastern

"I write meaty, honest copy that gets results without spamming, hyping, or hammering readers. Also, I always try to preserve the client's natural voice rather than imposing my own."

Specialization: Website copy that sells and press releases that attract media coverage.

BOOK PR SPECIALISTS

Publicity in the book industry is a rather different animal than publicity elsewhere, and since many of you either have or will have books, I've listed a few of the PR folks who work in that space.

Kate Siegel Bandos
KSB Promotions
kate@ksbpromotions   tel: 616-676-0758

http://www.ksbpromotions.com and http://www.ksblinks.com
Country/Time Zone: US/Eastern
"I find that we get the most pickups and requests by finding a key element of a book or a strong opinion of the author, and building a release around that point. We think any book or author should have multiple releases for multiple target markets."
Specialization: Press releases, supplemental releases, and author bios tied to books and authors.

Shel Horowitz
Accurate Writing & More
shel@principledprofits.com   tel: 413-586-2388 / 800-683-WORD
http://www.frugalmarketing.com
Country/Time Zone: US/Eastern
"It's not enough to say, 'I've published a book.' That happens over 120,000 times every year. I find the story behind the story, what makes your book special. Because I only write the copy and turn it back to you for distributing the material and following it up, I can provide very affordable professional copywriting to book authors and publishers."
Specialization: News releases/press releases, media pitch letters, GuestFinder/RTIR pages, Web pages, direct-mail, print ads (including classifieds), brochures, newsletters.

Claire Kirch
Claire Kirch Publicity Services
clairekirch@aol.com   tel: 218-727-8373
Country/Time Zone: US/Central
"I speak extensively to the author and carefully read the book before drafting copy, in order to accurately capture the essence of what the author is trying to convey in his or her work. I don't believe in flashy gimmicks, I believe in subtle, yet powerful, turns of phrase that brilliantly convey the author's message to booksellers, media, and of course, readers. I also don't take on any clients unless I can put my heart and soul into writing dazzling copy to promote them and their work."
Specialization: I write press releases, back cover copy, promotional materials

copy.…I specialize in working with literary fiction titles, as well as women's issues (both fiction and nonfiction).

Resources to Become a Better Copywriter/Publicist on Your Own

(In addition to the many listed in the appendix of *Grassroots Marketing*)

Allen, Debbie (ed.). *Confessions of Shameless Internet Promoters* (Scottsdale, Ariz.: Success Showcase Publications, 2002). An anthology of Internet marketing and publicity success stories from some of the top names in online marketing. A follow-up to her earlier *Confessions of Shameless Promoters*. My article starts on page 86.

Eisenberg, Brian, Jeffrey Eisenberg, and Lisa T. Davis. *Persuasive Online Copywriting: How to Take Your Words to the Bank* (Austin: Wizard Academy Press, 2002). Examines the difference between online and offline copywriting, always looking at how to increase the conversion rate. Many specific examples of how to integrate this approach into both Web and e-mail copy.

Evoy, Ken, and Joe Robson. *Make Your Words Sell* <http://frugalfun.sitesell.com/myws/>. Another of Ken's huge and ultra-useful e-books. Step-by-step to creating irresistible online copywriting.

Horowitz, Shel. *Grassroots Marketing: Getting Noticed in a Noisy World* (White River Junction, Vt.: Chelsea Green, 2000). 306 pages, large-format paperback. Available directly from the author at: <http://www.frugalmarketing.com, 800-683-WORD/413-586-2388>. Includes an extensive section on copywriting, with numerous examples.

Levinson, Jay Conrad, Rick Frishman, and Jill Lublin. *Guerrilla Publicity* (Avon, Mass.: Adams Media, 2002). This latest book in the Guerrilla Marketing series is specifically on getting publicity. Lots of attention to how to work with the press.

Other Publicity Resources

PR Leads: A much less expensive reseller of Profnet, a service that connects journalists working on stories with sources for those stories. I've used this service to get coverage in the *New York Times*, *Fortune Small Business*, Microsoft's bCentral.com, *Woman's Day*, and numerous other major (and minor) media. Read about it in detail at: <http://www.frugalmarketing.com/prleads.shtml>.

Radio TV Interview Report: A magazine for talk-show hosts and producers. Speakers, entrepreneurs, authors, and other sources purchase ads, and RTIR writes the copy. <http://www.rtir.com>

GuestFinder: A website connecting talk-show hosts and producers with potential guests who pay a small yearly fee for a detailed Web page with sample questions, headline topics, seasonal tie-ins, and other benefits <http://www.guestfinder.com>.

Annie Jennings PR: A PR agency that charges only for actual media placements. Also offers a fabulous series of free tele-seminars on various aspects of media publicity. Write to Annie@anniejenningspr.com to get on her mailing list. <http://www.anniejenningspr.com>

Index

Shel Horowitz was still a teenager when he started doing publicity for grassroots community organizations with zero promotional budgets. With no money available for stamps, he used to hand-deliver press releases by bicycle. Trained as a journalist, he first became aware of the power of the news media when a local paper refused to print his meeting notices for a controversial group—but gave extensive news coverage to its refusal.

After finishing Antioch College at age 19, Shel grappled with organizing his own various career paths, and that led to a new direction: résumé and career services. Shel turned résumé writing into a marketing function; writing marketing copy was a natural extension. Now, for over twenty years, he's helped businesses, nonprofits, individuals and community groups refine their marketing strategy, make the most of free and low-cost marketing opportunities, and save money in traditional advertising. He became active on the Internet in 1994, and put up the first of his four websites in 1996.

Shel is a popular lecturer and radio/teleseminar guest who has spoken to business, nonprofit, and consumer audiences across the country and around the world. Four of Shel's six books are on marketing, as are many of his 1000+ articles; he's also written thousands of marketing documents for himself and his clients.

With his wife, Dina Friedman, and children Alana and Rafael, he lives in a historic farmhouse in Hadley, Massachusetts.

To order additional copies of this book, or Shel's earlier book, *Grassroots Marketing: Getting Noticed in a Noisy World*, please visit:

<http://www.principledprofits.com>

<http:/www.frugalmarketing.com>

or call:

800-683-WORD/413-586-2388.

Bulk discounts are available. You may also order through your favorite bookstore.

You're also invited to visit Shel's sites to sign up for his free monthly marketing e-newsletters, *Positive Power of Principled Profit* and *Frugal Marketing Tips*, and to read the more than 900 free articles on marketing, entrepreneurship and lifestyles.